Ghosts of Derby

Ghosts of Derby

Wayne Anthony
&
Richard Felix

The Breedon Books
Publishing Company
Derby

First published in Great Britain by
The Breedon Books Publishing Company Limited
Breedon House, 44 Friar Gate, Derby, DE1 1DA.
1995

All houses where in men have lived and died are haunted houses.
Longfellow

Acknowledgements
The authors would like to thank all the people who have so willingly opened their hearts, homes and, more frequently, their business properties whilst research for this book was under way. A special thank you is due to all the people of Derby, including the many hundreds who have walked the streets of the city on the numerous ghost walks run from the Heritage Centre, who have also contributed stories and little known facts which are included in this book.

The authors are particularly grateful to their respective wives and families for their support, encouragement and understanding, and to the staff of the Local Studies Library in Iron Gate for their help and assistance. Special thanks are due to Cecilia Hannah Moore for her expertise in psychic-phenomena, to Betty Taylor for typing Richard's text, to Maxwell Craven for allowing access to Derby Museum's photographs, and to Amanda Volley for her advice and listening ear, and to the *Derby Evening Telegraph*, the *Derby Express*, the *Derby Trader* and the *Derbyshire Now* magazine, for their help in highlighting Derby as England's probable 'Ghost Capital'. The *Derby Evening Telegraph* also kindly loaned photographs.

ISBN 1 85983 042 0

Printed and bound by Butler & Tanner Limited, Selwood Printing Works, Caxton Road, Frome, Somerset.

Colour separations by Colour Services, Wigston, Leicester.

Jacket printed by Premier Print, Nottingham.

Contents

Foreword

UNTIL one or two enthusiastic authors recently started to write books on the ghostly mysteries of some of the Midland cities, this area, in the spectral sense at any rate, had been virtually fallow ground. It is good to see that the areas concerned are at long last having their spectral secrets revealed to what I know will be an enthusiastic band of readers.

The ground for ghost hunting here would appear to be exceptionally fruitful, and every nook and cranny in the ancient city of Derby seems to harbour its own ghostly occupants.

To satisfy the insatiable desires of large numbers of the population to seek out their own ghostly mysteries, a few words of salutary guidance may not go amiss.

The study of ghosts may be of interest to both folklorists and psychical researchers alike, so there is in reality a two-pronged approach to the subject. The folklorist will try to find stories that have been handed down from generation to generation by word of mouth, and will record them so that they might be preserved for prosperity. He will also conduct research into local history and traditions and will endeavour to discover whether any historical event of long ago might have inspired the stories in the first place. The psychical researcher will investigate cases of apparently inexplicable phenomena, sometimes happening at the present time that may be brought to his attention and for which he will always try to find a rational explanation.

It is essential, when carrying out a psychical investigation, not to be over-enthusiastic and jump to supernatural conclusions. It is always essential to try to find a natural cause for any inexplicable emanations by process of elimination, before arriving at the final possible conclusion. Climatic changes can often cause ancient timbers to contract and expand, often creating a sound not unlike a human footstep. Sounds of this sort, often heard in historical or modern buildings, should not make one convince oneself that the souls of the departed are not trying to re-assert themselves.

When seeking permission to carry out vigils in reputedly haunted places – and this should always be done before investigators commence their operations – every care and attention should be paid to the property to be investigated.

The highest form of rapport with those who believe themselves to be haunted can best be obtained by treating any information given in the strictest confidences, as in the confessional, and these confidences should never be revealed to the media without necessary permission. even though at times the blandishments of the media are difficult to ignore. The world of ghosts, in fact the whole realm of the paranormal, can be both an absorbing and a fascinating one, but whoever may be tempted into enveloping themselves in the spectral clouds, must, at the same time, place their feet firmly on the earth beneath.

Cities like Derby have survived the passage of time, despite the constant changes in the population. Old buildings have been demolished and new ones have been erected in their place. If the ethereal world of ghosts and phantoms really exists, spirits will remain with us for a long time to come, never failing to evoke the curiosity of those whose main objective in life is to fathom the enigmatic depths of the unknown in an effort to discover their existence.

Tom Perrott.
Chairman of The Ghost
Club (founded 1862)
London, September 1995

Preface

THIS book primarily serves as a guide book to places in Derby which have been, at some point in time, said to be haunted. It is impossible to ascertain whether all the stories are true, although most of the tales have been researched and it would appear that the majority of people who willingly gave their stories had, so far as the subject of ghosts is concerned, no axe to grind.

As to what ghosts actually are, well, this has puzzled mankind since the beginning of recorded history as ghosts appear in every civilisation and culture. There are obviously many sceptics, and just as many people who are embarrassed to admit their beliefs for fear of being ridiculed. In my experience, when people question my beliefs, perhaps with a view to ridiculing the subject, it is nearly always the case that they are themselves seeking to believe. My reply always tends to be the same: I simply state that only those who have truly loved and lost someone dear to them, have the right to look into their hearts and say whether life continues. Many individuals are increasingly losing their way in an age of disillusionment which is rapidly becoming a digital realm of cold computers.

There are many theories as to why ghosts exist and it seems that some of these may be the answers to some of the ghosts featured in this book, but most certainly not all. There is no single theory to explain all ghostly appearances as most of the evidence concerning this subject increasingly suggests that there is more than one type. One interesting theory, now accepted by many serious research-

Wayne Anthony, member of a family of practising mediums.

ers in the subject, is that of 'Electrical Impulse Wave Theory'. It is known that during a period of extreme emotional stress, brain waves (which can be recorded on an electro-

Photographic impressions of what a ghost may look like. The first picture purports to show a ghostly serving maid outside the Bell Hotel in Sadler Gate.
The other shows an impression of the white lady who is said to haunt the steps behind Derby Cathedral.

encephalograph) become more active. When these brain waves reach a certain pitch it is further believed that ordinary fabrics of buildings, bricks, mortar, furniture and so on electrically record them. Some time later, often years hence, certain people of a sensitive nature are able to briefly glimpse these often tragic recordings from the past. This seems feasible as the vast majority of recorded hauntings concern the ghosts of people who have in some way met with a tragic or violent death.

On many occasions, too numerous to mention here, I have heard the proprietor of an alleged haunted building state that they have lived at the building for many years and 'never seen anything' – in other words they don't believe – and until an apparition appears to them personally they never will. While this may well be true, it always strikes me as a rather sad statement because the answer as to whether one can, or will, ever see a ghost surely lies in the question of sensitivity – those who have the ability and those who do not. Admittedly the vast majority of sightings are by people who clearly state that they do not have a particular leaning towards the subject. In these instances I firmly believe that the individual, without knowing it, has dropped into another conscious mental state which briefly allows them to glimpse a ghost or a scene from an event long since passed.

To many people – especially visitors to the city – a book such as this should be considered as a supplement to the more material attractions which Derby has to offer. The book, apart from the obvious connection to ghosts, is also full of interesting and often little-known facts concerning the city of Derby. Much folklore and local legend has been included which hopefully will give the reader an interesting and extended insight into the city's broad history.

Finally it is worth remembering that when visiting places mentioned within this book it is best to observe the necessary proprieties when asking questions. Most people, I am sure, will only be too happy to answer any reasonable questions and, who knows, you might see or experience something not of this world.

Wayne Anthony
September 1995.

Introduction

ERBY'S location, almost in the centre of the country, has led to its great importance for almost 2,000 years, and also to its great prosperity. Lying where highland meets lowland, at the lowest crossing point of the River Trent and its contributory the Derwent, at the start of the Midlands plain and the end of the barren hills of the north, it has always been a crossing of the ways. Many people have passed through Derby on their way elsewhere; others have stayed. Some went on to greater things; others were dispatched whence they came.

Derby was the scene of the last hanging, drawing and quartering to be carried out in England, the result of the last rebellion against the Crown to take place in England. At one time or another there were five prisons in Derby – and a public house for every 36 people, no wonder there was a need for so many prisons. Derby also witnessed the last pressing to death, or the sentence of penance, which took place at the time of King Charles II in 1665. The only peer of the realm to be hanged for murder was Lawrence Shirley, 4th Earl Ferrers. For 126 years, the De Ferrers family were Earls of

Richard Felix in ghostly mood at the Derby Heritage Centre.

Mr and Mrs Gilbert of the Spiritualist Church in Forester Street, Derby, pictured around World War One with, according to a current member of the church, a returned spirit behind them. Such photographs were common at this time but the authors of this book were surprised when this copy print was developed and the figure of a man also appears to be between Mr and Mrs Gilbert, which was not clear on the original. The publishers, however, feel that this is maybe a stain on the picture which could be interpreted in this way.

Derby. Lawrence Shirley was also the first man in England to be hanged by the 'new drop' instead of the old system of the condemned standing on a cart with a noose round his or hers neck.

Mary, Queen of Scots, on her way to be executed at Fotheringhay Castle, slept in Derby; the hopes and aspirations of Bonnie Prince Charlie foundered here; Florence Nightingale went on from Derby Railway Station to world fame.

No wonder then – with Derby's long and illustrious history – that there are so many souls still lingering here.

I strongly believe that ghosts, spirits and hauntings can play a very real part in telling the story of an historic city like Derby. Many of the hauntings and the sightings within the city have been influenced by the events which have happened here, at Derby, truly the crossroads of history.

People say that ghosts do not know that they are dead, and that in the trauma just before death, the energy expelled or expounded is for some reason absorbed into the building – the stonework, the woodwork – and for some reason, at certain times the events immediately prior to their death can be recalled or replayed, just as today the button on a video recorder can be switched to play and, behold, we can watch someone long dead appear on a screen.

Buildings, of course, change, and when a ghost is reported to be 'legless' it is often because the floor became higher; if they are headless, unless, of course, their head is seen tucked under their arm, it is because the ceiling is now lower than at the time of their death. Many people have seen ghosts 'walk through the walls' – are they really going through the wall or was there a door there? Has it now been bricked up and plastered over and wall paper put over it? Is the ghost simply going through a door as it once knew it?

Perhaps I am the wrong person to be writing books on ghosts, talking to people about ghosts and leading ghost walks around the city of Derby. As a child I was petrified of ghosts and, to a certain extent, to this day I still am, although the only experience I can claim was when I heard the disembodied voice of a young man dying of his wounds in Bestwood Lodge, Nottingham, in 1976. When I was four years of age I was locked into garages and garden sheds by friends and told that the 'Green Ghost' was going to get me. Many a night, when I was a child, did I lay awake beneath my bedclothes at night with my fingers crossed waiting for that sighting, waiting for that demonic being to enter my bedroom, pull back the bedclothes and reveal its hideous face. Of course this never happened.

As a child I would not go upstairs alone, nor would I stay in any building alone, and I would certainly not walk past a graveyard alone. This fear is, again to a certain extent, still with me today. Like so many people, of course, when someone is with me I am not afraid, but when left alone in the dark, with my innermost thoughts, those ghostly memories from my childhood come flooding back.

Richard Felix
September 1995

Tormented Souls

Haunted Derby Gaols

The earliest gaol recorded at Derby was in the vicinity of Markeaton Brook near the junction of St Peter's Street and the Corn Market. This prison was in use about the middle of the 16th century and continued in

St Peter's Bridge with Markeaton Brook flowing underneath it. Both the bridge and the brook are now out of sight under the modern roadway, but in 1610 three prisoners in the old Derby Gaol near here were drowned when the brook overflowed.

use until 1756. William Hutton, writing *A History of Derby* in 1791, records how three prisoners were drowned there in 1610 when the brook, which was still open at that time, flooded one night causing the men's deaths.

Some 150 years after this event it was decided that a new

The old Derby Borough Gaol which stood where the former Howard Hotel in Friar Gate is now situated. It was a grim place where many prisoners awaited execution for relatively minor crimes, often committed simply to feed their families.

gaol would be built and an appropriate site was chosen at Nun's Green, the prison occupying what was later Nos 47 to 51 Friar Gate, where the Howard Hotel now stands. It was erected in 1756 by the Corporation and aided by a donation of £400 from the Duke of Devonshire. The result seems to have pleased many people, for the gaol was described as being a 'solid and respectable building of brick'. The Friar Gate prison was in use as the Derby Borough Gaol from 1827 until 1840, after which prisoners were kept at the County Gaol in Vernon Street, which was built in 1827.

Almost every property in the Friar Gate area of Derby seems to have an indwelling spirit which has been seen at sometime or another over the last 100 years. More and more stories are coming out of the area all of the time and it is often difficult to keep records of which property is haunted by which type of spirit. Perhaps it is not so unusual that this area, with its colourful and often tragic history, should have so many ghosts and spectres.

Once we delve into the history of Friar Gate we begin to uncover a fascinating multitude of different personalities and classes of people who have, through the centuries, left their mark upon the area.

Several students from Derby University had decided, as part of their religious studies course, to study ghosts and had arranged to visit the Howard Hotel to see if they could capture a ghost on film or even record any strange happenings. They had heard of the building's reputation for being haunted and decided that this would be a good place to conduct a serious investigation into the supernatural. I was asked if I would like to go along for the experience, an offer which I must admit I jumped at. The night was arranged with the tenant, who had already experienced strange happenings, even though she had only been there a short time.

The basement beneath the Howard Hotel has housed several different clubs over the past 20 years and has recently been turned into yet another club offering merriment and music in what was once a place where people walked to their deaths. The condemned cells, where prisoners who were to be executed were kept prior to being taken to the gallows, still retain their original doors upon which many of the ill-fated criminals inscribed their initials and the date they were to be executed. One wonders how these criminals must have felt in their dank, dark, tiny cubicles, half starved and having only straw upon which to rest their often emaciated bodies. The despair and anguish which these men and women must have experienced is hard to imagine and if the walls, floors and other fabric of the building could

speak, I am sure that they would have many a sorry, tragic and often gruesome tale to tell.

The night had been long awaited and I had anticipated that there was going to be a great deal happening to prove that the club, which we were

Cells of the Borough Gaol beneath the former Howard Hotel. The basement has been turned into a club but most of the original cell doors are still in place. The door pictured at the far end of this small corridor originally guarded the condemned cell and there are still carvings on the door, giving the initials and dates of execution of condemned men, some grimly showing the gallows as well. Alas, this historic fabric is now simply leaning against this blank wall and one modern-day patron of the basement has already scratched his name on it. One cannot help but feel that this important part of Derby's heritage should be in a museum or at least properly protected. Having survived unscathed for two centuries it is now prey to modern vandalism.

visiting, was indeed haunted by spirits still not at rest. I had visited the club on several occasions before and had experienced, along with many other people, strange happenings and spirit sightings along with unexplained chanting noises and groans which seemed to come from nowhere.

My first visit to the property was eight years before, when it was being converted and was still known as the Howard Hotel. I was originally alerted to the fact that there were alleged spirits in the Howard Hotel basement by an article in the *Derby Evening Telegraph* which reported that workmen converting the building had reported seeing a strange caped figure and phosphorous lights in the vicinity of the old condemned cells in what was once the Derby Borough Gaol, where prisoners had awaited execution, sometimes for the mere crime of stealing a loaf of bread to feed their starving families.

When I arrived at the club there were already about ten people there, several of whom claimed to be psychic, or sensitive to ghosts in some way. We were organised into small groups and told to sit in different parts of the club. I chose to sit in what was once a condemned cell where, I was informed, most of the ghostly happenings had taken place. We were further told to change locations about every 30 minutes and to record any strange occurrences. After the allocated time was up we were told to change locations and begin the process yet again.

What followed next will seem hard to believe, although all the people, of which there were eventually 11, experienced the same phenomenon. We had not long settled into our second positions and had divided into twos. Several home video recorders were in use as well as several thermometers as many ghost sightings seem to correspond with sudden drops in temperature often resulting in an icy chill referred to by many people in the area of ghost hunting as 'cold spots'.

Suddenly there was a loud cry from one of our party and we all rushed to the area, which happened to be another cell, to see what was happening. When we arrived there, a lady called Sue was being comforted by another lady who informed us all that Sue was claiming to have been taken over by the spirit of a man who was once an executioner. Most of the people were sceptical and obviously found this hard to believe. All of a sudden Sue jumped up from where she was sitting and began stamping her feet, describing what she claimed this man wanted. What she told us was that the spirit of the executioner was not at rest and could not rest, for he was bound to this world through the guilt that he was carrying.

Eventually we managed to settle Sue down and continue with the vigil. Soon after we had all retaken our places, strange noises began to be heard in the building. One lady claimed to have seen the ghost of a child, while another insisted that when she stood in a certain spot, she felt a strange 'chopping' feeling on her neck. Around three quarters of the group admitted that they too experienced this unpleasant feeling when they were standing in or near the area, which happened to be just a few feet away from the condemned cell. Many people also said that they could hear someone or something whistling; others claimed to have seen grey smoky figures.

As the night progressed there were many other smaller incidents including the sound of footsteps and a child crying. Shortly after midnight it was decided that a seance would be held in the hope that a ghost might

This door is still in place, affixed to one of the former cells beneath the former Howard Hotel. The carvings of prisoners held in this small, dank, dark room can be clearly seen. One, to the top right, is dated 1818.

materialise so that the students might capture it on film. No ghost appeared, although what did happen may also seem impossible to many people.

The room was dimly lit by a myriad of faintly flickering candles. Everyone was sitting in what we were told was the original guards' room where, we were also informed, the ghost of an old man with grey hair and a melancholy-looking face and wearing a brown leather waistcoat had frequently been seen. The atmosphere of the room seemed icy and a definite feeling of anticipation rippled throughout the group.

Christine, a researcher with the group, sat in a seat opposite to where everyone else was sitting. Then another member of the group noticed

that Christine's features had begun to visibly change.

One hitherto sceptical member of the group described to me exactly what they had seen several days after the event: "As I looked across the room my eyes were drawn to a lady sitting in a chair close to a fireplace where several candles were lit. As I gazed at her, it was as if suddenly a transparent opaque veil had been drawn across her face and at the same time I noticed that the rest of the room seemed to go hazy. The next thing I remember was that the face I had just been looking at now seemed not to be there. Instead there was the face of an old man with a short beard and much darker hair and with a moustache. I continued to stare for

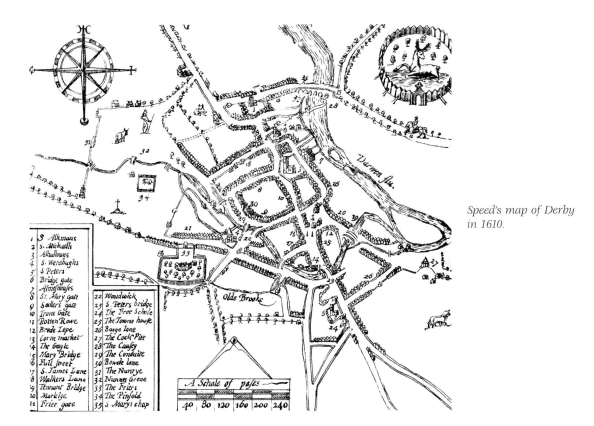

Speed's map of Derby in 1610.

The map legend reads:

1	S. Alkmans		
2	S. Michaells		
3	Alhallowes		
4	S. Werebughs		
5	S. Peters		
6	Bridge gate		
7	Almeshouses		
8	St. Mary gate	22	Wenidwick
9	Sadler's gate	23	S. Peters bridge
10	Irone Gate	24	The Free Schole
11	Rotten Rowe	25	The Towne house
12	Brode Iepe	26	Barge lane
13	Corne market	27	The Cock Pitt
14	The Gayle	28	The Causy
15	Mary Bridge	29	The Conduite
16	Full streete	30	Bowde lane
17	S. James Lane	31	The Nunrye
18	Walkers Lane	32	Nunnes Grene
19	Tennant Bridge	33	The Friers
20	Markeige	34	The Pinfold
21	Frier gate	35	S. Marys chap

A Schale of pases
40 80 120 160 200 240

several minutes and eventually drew several other people's attention to what was taking place.

"All the other members of the group also saw the same thing and we all watched fascinated by what was taking place. It seemed an impossible thing to have happened and many of us were shocked that it had. One might say that it was a trick of light, except for the fact that it did not happen just the once, several other people present sat in the same place and it happened again and again, sometimes with several other faces appearing in succession."

What the people had actually experienced was a phenomenon which many mediums refer to as 'transfiguration', where the faces of those who have died appear like a mask over selected individuals faces. This phenomenon can occasionally happen spontaneously although this, I am informed, is extremely rare. This appears to be what happened that night. Even a reporter from the *Derby Evening Telegraph*, who also happened to sit in the same place, transfigured into a young boy.

The exact process of a transfiguration is complex and involves a substance known as ectoplasm, which derives its name from the Greek words *ektos* and *plasma*, meaning 'exteriorised substance'.

S.G.Soal, in his book *A Survey of the Occult* (1935), writes: "Some observers describe it as being inert, while others declare that it squirms and wriggles to mould itself into hands and heads and even into complete forms of animals and human beings. . . .It is a most chameleon-like form of matter."

Ectoplasm is said to be extruded from the ears, mouth, nostrils or genitals of mediums or potential psychics whilst in a trance-like state. Other people in the vicinity are also said to contribute from their own bodily secretions and there has been much debate over this substance over the last century. Many mediums who claim to bring forth this kind of phenomenon have been exposed as fakes, although there are still numerous mediums who still manage to astound the experts.

The night continued and at one point we could all hear what appeared to be monks singing. There were also numerous knocks and rapping noises, the sound of shuffling feet and at one point the candles point dimmed of their own accord. Sue, who had experienced being taken over by the spirit of an executioner, managed to settle herself, although she still seemed a little shaky. By 3.30am we were all extremely tired and decided to call it a night. Eventually we all drifted away, the majority of us convinced that we had just spent the last five hours in a very haunted building. **W.A.**

The Agard Street Apparition

A bloody murder took place in court No 4 Agard Street on 13 February 1862, witnessed by a ten-year-old boy, disturbed from quietly playing by the sounds of two adults, one male, one female, arguing. As the young boy watched he saw the man take out a shiny instrument and lunge for the woman who screamed and staggered back clutching a bloody throat. The man then ran off into Agard Street, leaving his victim bleeding to death with the instrument of her demise, a 'cut-throat razor', lying beside her.

A local surgeon, Doctor Joseph German, was summoned to the scene and arrived there shortly afterwards, but was unable to help the young lady as the lacerations to her neck and face were so severe and she expired her last breath in Dr German's arms.

The woman was Eliza Morrow and her former lover, Richard Thorley, was her killer. The boy was Charles Wibberly, whose testimony was to play a crucial part in securing the conviction of the man who was to suffer Derby's last public execution. Two other ladies, Urania Morrow, probably a relative, and Emma Underwood, also claimed to have seen the murder committed and informed Inspector Fearn of the Derby Constabulary that it was Richard Thorley.

Thorley had been courting Eliza Morrow since the death of his wife several months previously. The relationship seems to have been a stormy one, the two regularly arguing over trivial issues and on one occasion Thorley blacking Eliza's eye. Thorley was in the habit of giving Eliza money, which at first she seemed to appreciate as the meagre wage she earned as a mill hand was hardly enough to sustain her. Eventually Eliza became tired of Thorley's constant attentions and started seeing a soldier, much to

Children from Derby's old West End, pictured in the 1870s. A few years earlier one such youngster had been the star witness at a murder trial after a brutal crime in Agard Street.

Thorley's annoyance. He had an extremely jealous, possessive nature and, finding it hard to accept that Eliza no longer wished to see him, he resorted to following her around. Eventually he decided to confront Eliza and try to persuade her to give up the soldier. Eliza was having none of it, perhaps because she had become frightened of the increasingly aggressive Thorley. The two argued and Thorley produced a razor and cut her throat.

Running from the court in Agard Street, Thorley made his way to the Spa Inn on Abbey Street where he purchased two bottles of ginger beer and drank them both. The landlord, Thomas Chapman, noticed that Thorley's hands were covered in blood-stained bandages. The landlord questioned Thorley, who explained that he had been involved in a fight with an Irishman in the Abbey Inn further down Abbey Street. Finishing his drink, Thorley bid the landlord goodnight and left.

Shortly after midnight he was apprehended in Canal Street by Detective-Sergeant Vessey, who told Thorley that he was arresting him for committing the murder of Eliza Morrow, to which Thorley replied: "I have done it. I cannot help it now. I am sorry." Thorley was taken to the Lock-Up off the Cornmarket before being transferred to the County Gaol in Vernon Street where he awaited trial.

Thorley did not have long to wait,

The County Gaol in Vernon Street. The last public execution was carried out in front of these walls which still stand, perhaps haunted by the ghost of the murderer Richard Thorley.

for his trial was set for 24 March 1862, only six weeks after Eliza Morrow had been killed. He appeared before Mr Justice Williams. Thorley's defence council, Mr Yeatman QC, questioned the witnesses intently, particularly young Charles Wibberly, who stuck to his story under close cross-examination. Mr Yeatman argued that Eliza's death should be classed as one of manslaughter, as it occurred in a moment of haste and passion. Judge Justice Williams, however, was not convinced and advised the jury not to consider the crime as an act of passion, but as one of murder.

The jury did not take long to consider the evidence and quickly returned a verdict of guilty. Asked if he had anything to say, Thorley replied: "What I have to say will amount to nothing, since three

witnesses have spoken falsely against me."

Justice Williams donned the black cap and passed the death sentence, condemning Richard Thorley to be executed at noon on 11 April 1862. The convicted murderer was then led away from the dock.

In the early hours of the morning, on the day of his execution, Thorley wrote out a full confession. He told the prison chaplain that he had no regrets and stated that 'she got what she deserved'. At 9.30am the condemned service was held in Thorley's cell. Shortly before noon, a bell tolled to signify that execution was at hand, and Thorley said goodbye to his fellow inmates with the words, "Let my sentence be a warning to you all."

Many more details concerning Richard Thorley's life were to emerge

The former County Gaol in Vernon Street. A screaming ghost also haunts the area.

whilst he was awaiting execution. Thorley was born in the Leather Bottle Yard, Osmaston Street, now Osmaston Road. He had worked throughout his life in local foundries, his last employer giving him a character reference during his trial, at which it was stated that 'Thorley had been a conscientious hard worker, who had shown much concern and sensitivity to his wife during the illness which eventually resulted in her death'.

He was also well-known as a local prize-fighter and it would appear that he had much success in this area. In his last letter, an open one written to the Derby newspapers, Thorley rejected his life-style stating that he was 'too fond of gambling, and the ale house, and though I am now almost ashamed to confess it, that I was one of the fraternity styling themselves the Derby Fancy'.

It is estimated that between 10,000 and 15,000 people gathered outside the walls of the prison in Vernon Street to watch what was to be Derby's last public execution. Many people had travelled from far and wide, many having arrived early in order to obtain a good view of the execution. The spectators were hushed as Thorley mounted the scaffold, his pale face turned upward and his lips moving fervently in prayer. He handed a small hymn book to one of the officials. In it were words inscribed for his sister: "Hannah Brearley, with her brother Thorley's dying love, April 11th 1862". The noose was then placed around his neck by executioner Calcraft and within seconds the deed was done.

Thorley's body was left hanging for a full hour before being cut down and buried within the prison walls. Never was Derby to witness such a barbaric public execution again, even though private executions would still continue into the next century.

Not long after the trial and execution of Richard Thorley, strange stories of ghosts and spectres that rattled chains and bewailed their outcast state emerged from Agard Street, stories which continued into the present century. Workers at a former factory on Agard Street were familiar with the story of Thorley and Eliza. Many claimed to have seen a lady in blue wandering the premises, whilst others swore that they had heard the phantom sounds of rattling chains.

After an appeal on BBC Radio Derby by myself and Richard Felix, I received a telephone call from a lady named Carol, who informed me that her mother was once employed as a factory worker at Longden's Fabric Spinners in Agard Street. Carol reiterated to me the story which her mother had been told when she worked at the factory.

"Most workers at the factory were familiar with the murder story concerning Richard Thorley and Eliza Morrow. So frequent were the ghostly sightings of a lady in blue and a gentleman who moaned and rattled chains that the workers at the factory referred to the two ghosts as "Lizzy and Dick". Many people, including my mother, experienced strange occurrences in the upper regions of the factory. One particular day my mother was working upstairs in the factory when she glanced up from her work and noticed the shadowy figure of a lady in blue move across the room and walk through the wall."

Carol went on to say that there appears to have always been a reputation, for many of the buildings in Agard Street to be haunted by these two spirits. Even during World War Two rumours abounded of strange sightings of Richard Thorley, whose ghostly image was said to be seen dragging his prison chains behind him. The sombre figure of Eliza has also been occasionally glimpsed, especially by one local gentleman, returning home from an evening out, when he came face to face with what he believed to be the 'ghostly figure of Eliza Morrow', who, looked directly into his eyes and then vanished.

Over the last few years many new buildings have sprung up in Agard Street. It will be interesting to know whether these tragic ghost stories of the two lovers will continue to circulate, perhaps being added to by new stories and appearances which may yet take place.   **W.A.**

Shire Hall, St Mary's Gate

"That you be taken back to the prison whence you came to a low dungeon, into which no light can enter; that you be laid on your back on the bare floor with a cloth around your loins but elsewhere naked; that there be set upon your body a weight of iron as great as you can bear and greater; that you have no sustenance except on the first day a morsel of coarse bread and on the second day three draughts of stagnant water from the pool nearest the prison door and on the third another morsel of coarse bread as before. If after three days you are still alive the weight will be taken from your body and a large sharp stone placed beneath your back and the weight replaced."

A deaf mute woman was thus sentenced in the Shire Hall, St Mary's

Forbidding looking court room in the Shire Hall.

Gate, and pressed to death in 1665. Accused persons who remained in the witness box in court were given three chances to plead guilty or not guilty. After the third time of asking, followed by time for reconsideration, 'judgement of penance' was passed – the above blood curdling sentence.

This was the last time in England that this horrible execution was carried out and her ghost is said to still wander in the cells which are preserved

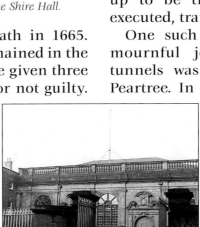
The Shire Hall in St Mary's Gate. In the mid-17th century the last sentence in England of 'pressing to death' was read out here.

underneath Derby's Shire Hall, possibly the most ominous building remaining in Derby to this day. It was built in 1659 and was the scene of all the famous murder trials in Derbyshire. The Pentrich Martyrs were sentenced to be hanged, drawn and quartered there in 1817. That was the last time such a sentence was passed in England. **R.F.**

Guildhall Catacombs

Beneath Derby's Guildhall is a labyrinth of tunnels and catacombs. One of the tunnels used to link the old police lock-up in Lock-Up Yard to the Assize Courts which were at that time in the Guildhall. Many prisoners have trudged along those dark, dank tunnels from the lock-up to the courts, where they were sentenced, and then trudged back into the lock-up to be then taken away to be executed, transported, or imprisoned.

One such person who made the mournful journey through those tunnels was Alice Wheeldon, from Peartree. In 1917 it was alleged that she had plotted to murder David Lloyd George, the Prime Minister. She was arrested in Pear Tree Road, Derby, taken to the lock-up and eventually tried at the Assize Courts.

People say that they still hear ghostly footsteps along those tunnels. Perhaps it is those of Alice Wheel-

The Guildhall in Derby Market Place pictured around the turn of the century. Underneath are tunnels which linked the Assize Courts to the Lock-Up.

don, who although imprisoned, was later found to be innocent. The whole story was apparently fabricated by the British Government because Alice Wheeldon was hiding Conscientious Objectors – men who did not wish to fight as soldiers– in World War One. She was later released from prison and lived as a recluse in Derby until she died and was then buried in an unmarked grave somewhere in the town. Also within the Guildhall catacombs, the ghost of a little boy has been seen, dressed in rags. He often wanders through the tunnels and has been seen by workmen. They shout at him, thinking that he is trespassing, but then he disappears and although thorough searches are undertaken, no sign of the boy can be found. **R.F.**

Historical Ghosts

Babington Lane and Mary, Queen of Scots

Babington Lane in Derby is named after the Babingtons of Dethick, a family of wealthy lead miners. On the corner of Babington Lane and St Peter's Street today stand the Babington Buildings, on the gable of which is the family crest – a baboon on a tun or barrel signifying 'Babington'.

Across the road from the Babington Buildings, until 1826, stood Babington Hall, town house of Sir Anthony Babington. At the age of ten Babington had been made a ward of the 6th Earl of Shrewsbury, fourth husband of Bess of Hardwick. Shrewsbury and his wife were the joint custodians of Mary, Queen of Scots, Stuart Pretender to the English throne. Babington became a page to Mary and was infatuated with her. Like her, he was a Catholic and believed, as did the rest of the Catholic world, that she was the rightful Queen

Mary, Queen of Scots who spent on night in Derby. Her ghost has been seen in Babington Lane as well as other places in Derbyshire.

of England, not her Protestant cousin, Elizabeth – they were both grandchildren of Henry VII – who Catholics regarded as illegitimate.

In a bid to bring this about, Babington plotted with other Catholic conspirators and invited King Phillip II of Spain to send an army to invade England – as he eventually attempted in 1588 when the Armada foundered. Babington planned to murder Queen Elizabeth and put Mary, Queen of Scots on the throne of England. Tragically for the conspirators, Sir Francis Walsingham, Elizabeth's 'spy catcher', uncovered the plot after intercepting letters between Babington and Mary, which were sent from various places such as Tutbury Castle and Chartley Manor via a Burton brewer who smuggled the letters in a water-tight barrel. Using the information from the so-called Babington Plot, Walsingham gathered enough evidence to have Mary, Queen of Scots tried for treason and condemned to

The corner of Babington Lane and St Peter's Street. Mary, Queen of Scots' ghost has been sighted near here.

The ghost of Sir Anthony Babington is alleged to haunt Manor Farm, Dethick.

death. In the years leading up to her fate she had been imprisoned in many parts of England including Derbyshire, being incarcerated no less than five times at the old Chatsworth House (in 1570, 1573, 1577, 1578 and 1581), where the Earl of Shrewsbury, was her gaoler. He first received custody of the queen in January 1565 at Tutbury Castle. Two months later she was removed to Wingfield Manor and later was taken to Chatsworth. All in all, the captive queen was manoeuvred to many parts of Derbyshire and Staffordshire, her most hated place of captivity being Tutbury Castle which she described as 'exposed to all the winds and "injuries" of heaven'.

On the night of 13 January 1585, Mary's coach had trundled across little St Mary's Bridge, the only bridge over the River Derwent into Derby, taking her up St Peter's Street to the home of Sir Anthony Babington. The unfortunate Mary was being taken from Wingfield Manor to Tutbury Castle and she spent her last night in Derbyshire in Babington Hall – ironically, in the home of the man whose desire to see her as Queen of England would end in her execution.

On arriving at Babington Hall, Queen Mary was greeted by her hostess, Mrs Beaumont, at which stage the queen is said to have remarked: "Having no husbands to trouble us, we should get on well together". Mrs Beaumont had arranged for the queen to be entertained lavishly by several of her neighbours. Sir Ralph Sadler, who was to deliver her to Tutbury Castle, was later called upon by Queen Elizabeth to explain these actions. Lodged in a nearby inn, Sir Ralph later complained that he had been kept awake most of the night by Derby watchmen calling the hour beneath his bedroom window.

Later that year, Babington, John Ballard (a Catholic priest of Rheims and Babington's main co-conspirator) and five other men were tried before a special

Tutbury Castle, where Mary, Queen of Scots was taken after spending the night in Derby.

commission. Babington attempted to lay the blame on Ballard and wrote to Queen Elizabeth beseeching her to work a miracle of mercy upon him and spare his life. To a friend he promised the sum of £1,000 if his release could be obtained. This was to no avail and on 20 September 1585, Babington, Ballard and their five co-conspirators were taken to St Giles's in London where they were hanged, drawn and quartered. Anthony Babington declared from the scaffold that no private ends had influenced him and he believed his part in the plot to be 'a deed lawful and meritorious'. Mary was executed 17 months later at Fotheringhay Castle in Northamptonshire on 8 February 1587. Her body was first buried in

Peterborough Cathedral but when her son ascended the English throne as King James I, he had it removed to Westminster Abbey where it lies today beneath a magnificent white marble monument.

For many years people working in the various offices that now occupy the site of Derby's Babington Hall have sensed an unearthly presence when they are alone in the rooms there. Could this be the ghost of the unfortunate Mary Stuart, still lingering to this day near the home of the man so central to her fate? That ghostly coach which brought her to Derby has also occasionally been seen on the anniversary of Mary Stuart's only night in the town.

Indeed, shortly after Mary had been beheaded in the Great Hall of Fotheringhay Castle – executioner Simon Bull apparently took three blows to sever her head with his axe – rumours began to circulate that her ghost had been seen wandering through several of the houses and castles in which she had been imprisoned. Many of the houses within Derbyshire and Staffordshire still hold firm to the belief that her ghost walks their corridors and halls.

At Chatsworth House in Derbyshire

The Babington Tree at Wingfield Manor, said to have grown from a walnut dropped by Sir Anthony Babington when he visited Mary, Queen of Scots.

there is a raised summer house which is known to be one of the many places where Mary, Queen of Scots was imprisoned. It is here, as well as at Wingfield Manor, and the site where Babington Hall once stood on Babington Lane that the ghost of the ill-fated queen has been seen with a forlorn look about her. The raised summer house at Chatsworth – known as Queen Mary's Bower – is believed to have been specially built for her, as it bears her coat-of-arms above the iron gateway at the top of the stairs.

Sir Anthony Babington, it is said, frequently stole into Wingfield Manor to see Mary, who was held in the tower there. Legend says that he used to disguise himself by rubbing the oil of walnuts on to his skin, which stained the flesh, giving him the appearance of someone much older. One particular night, while sneaking past the guards, Babington was disturbed by a patrolling soldier and, in his haste to get out of sight, dropped from his pocket a walnut, which over a period of time seeded itself and grew into a great walnut tree which may still be seen within the ruins today.

The ghosts of the two would-be lovers still haunt the grounds of the manor, there being several people, including one couple, who swear that they have encountered the two walking in the grounds. The iron bars and guards that may have kept them apart while flesh clung to their bones has no power to do the same in death.

W.A. & R.F.

Bonnie Prince Charlie, reluctantly turned back from Derby and now haunts the place of where his dream of taking the English crown was crushed.

Derby and the Young Pretender

Some 160 years after the tragic Mary, Queen of Scots spent one night in Derby, the last Stuart Pretender to the throne of England reached a crossroad of history in the town. Bonnie Prince Charlie was Mary, Queen of Scots' great, great, great, great grandson and on 4 December 1745, he arrived in Derby on his way to London and an attempt to take crown. His 5,500 troops doubled the size of the town for the three days they were in occupation.

Charles Edward Stuart took up his quarters in Exeter House in Full Street, where the Police Station now

The Bonnie Prince Charlie Room at Derby Museum, as it looked before refurbishment. Do the panels of this room hold secrets from the night that the Young Pretender unsuccessfully argued the case against retreat?

stands. His officers and their soldiers were billeted in houses and inns around the town. Two government armies were converging on Derby and after a heated argument that went on long into the night, Prince Charlie's generals and clan chiefs decided that their cause was all but lost. There was no English support for them and so retreat was their only option.

Exeter House was demolished in 1854, but the panelling from the drawing room where that fateful decision was made is housed in Derby Museum, in what is now known as the Bonnie Prince Charlie Room.

Charles had tried everything within his power to persuade his officers to go on from Derby. "I see nothing but ruin and destruction before us if we do not go on from this place," he said, but they would not change their minds.

His manipulative powers were waning. "I would rather be twenty feet under the ground than go back," he said, but still his generals would not listen to him: they had made up their minds.

The prince stormed out of the room, and as he went he shouted back at them, "In future I will summon no more councils, as I am accountable to

Not the ghost of the Young Pretender but a 'high-tec' model of him in the Bonnie Prince Charlie Room as Derby Museum prepared to celebrate the 250th anniversary of his visit in December 1995.

no one but God and to my father the King!" Thus the hopes and aspirations of the Royal House of Stuart foundered in that room in Derby. There is a strange feeling of foreboding as one enters the room. The hopelessness, the despair that Charles Edward Stuart must have experienced some 250 years ago, appears to emanate from the reconstructed room's very panelling.   **R.F.**

Little Chester's Roman Ghosts

There is much evidence to suggest that as early as 80AD, a Roman fort existed besides the River Derwent, at Little Chester, which the Romans called Derventio. Archaeological excavations of the site revealed that the defences of the fort were rectangular in shape, enclosing an estimated area of seven acres, being surrounded by two deep ditches placed 100ft apart. A clay rampart was later added, and later still the site was reinforced with a thick stone wall some 10ft to 15ft high.

The playing field and car-park at the junction of City Road and Old Chester Road is probably where the main headquarters building stood. It is also thought that several other buildings occupied the site, including an infirmary, an armoury and other smaller units making the whole site of Little Chester self-sufficient.

Although no inscriptions have yet

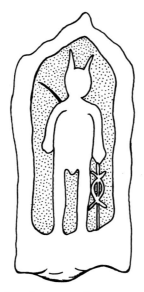

A drawing of the Mercury Stone which was found at Little Chester, perhaps a former pagan site which, according to some, still retains an air of mystery

Left and opposite page: Saxon remains at Little Chester. Could ghostly happenings there be connected with the disturbance of these bodies?

been found at Little Chester, there are references from other ancient sources where the later name Derbentione, appears between Lutudarum and Salinae in a seventh-century town listings (the *Ravenna Cosmography*). The only indication as to how many soldiers were stationed on the site lies in the size of the fort, which covered seven acres and therefore had to have housed one of the bigger auxiliary forts. The largest cavalry units (*Alla Milliaria*), meaning a thousand horsemen, was believed to be stationed in Britain, at Stanwix, on Hadrian's Wall. The unit appearing to be most suitably placed at Little Chester would have been a *Cohors Equitata Milliaria*, which consisted of ten centuries of infantry, and in total five of these units were stationed in Britain.

Much of the site at Little Chester has been excavated, although there is almost certainly a great deal yet to be uncovered. Some interesting finds, however, have surfaced at the site, amongst which is a gritstone block,

crudely carved in the shape of a shrine containing within it the nude figure of a horned man. This was found in the last century by a gardener digging near the River Derwent. This gritstone block, known as the Mercury Stone, has so far been the only carving found at the site, and although originally the figure was thought to represent the Roman god, Mercury, it is now believed to be the horned god of the Brigantes whose cult became combined with that of the Roman deity. The Mercury Stone is at present on display, at Derby Museum and Art Gallery. The carved stone figure is also believed by many to represent a horned god of fertility, worshipped by ancient pagans and still held sacred by modern-day witches.

In November 1978, a burial ground was discovered when trees and undergrowth were being removed by bulldozers on the Racecourse Playing Fields. This ancient graveyard is believed to have existed on the east side of the encampment as Roman

law stated that no burials, except those of young children, were allowed within town. Other burial grounds were also uncovered on the Racecourse. One particular grave site, containing both inhumations and cremations, had unusual features: several of the interments had been mutilated prior to or whilst being buried; the left hand of one had been severed; others had been decapitated and in several cases the heads had been placed between the knees; two others had been buried face down.

The reason for these strange rites at the time of burial perhaps dates back to an old superstitious belief concerning witches and dark sorcery. When a dead person was believed to have been a witch or black magician, or in any way connected with magic and witchcraft, it was the custom to bury them face down or remove their head in order that they should not rise from the grave and haunt the living. Another grave site, not far from where the mutilated remains were found, consisted of three male bodies, one of which was found to have two coins placed upon him. These coins were probably placed there in the belief that they would be accepted by the deity Charon, whose job it was to ferry the souls of the dead across the dark waters of the River Styx on their journey to the Underworld.

Many buildings at Chester Green, especially those buildings close to the remains of the excavated Roman encampment, are known to be haunted. One interesting story comes from a lady who lives in a house whose history probably dates back to a time when part of the building was used for storage by the Romans. Although the ghost has not made a personal appearance he, or she, has manifested themselves in other ways. The ghost frequently clears away household rubbish, closes opened curtains in the living room, and has been known on several occasions to wash dirty crockery, much to the appreciation of the owner.

Another instance, seemingly more frightening, is the appearance of a spectre which is said to resemble a Roman centurion. One Derby man claims to have seen this figure one dark, foggy winter's evening whilst walking home from work. "The ghost," I was informed, "just glared at me with very large eyes." This gentleman went on to state that-he had not waited about to question the apparition but had hurried home to the waiting comfort of his front room and a stiff drink.

Many times over the last decade, I have received requests from people living in the Chester Green area, who have asked me to investigate a haunting that they feel they might have. Several of these people had indeed disturbed forces within their homes, whilst others were perhaps suffering from over-active imaginations.

Other ghosts have been seen in the area, including a whole regiment of Roman soldiers, seen and heard marching one night near the River Derwent. The apparition of a ghostly child with snow-white hair has been observed near the site of a Roman well. One lady who has lived in the area for many years claims that the area of Little Chester has always had the reputation of being haunted by sinister things. This lady also claims that since excavations have been carried out in the area in 1978, even more ghosts have been seen. She further stated that the excavations has disturbed spirits which would of been best left untroubled, in what should of been their final resting places.

W.A.

The Black Death in Derby

There are probably more bodies in St Peter's Churchyard than in any other graveyard in Derby. St Peter's was once the most densely populated part of Derby and when the Black Death struck the town in 1349, more people died in St Peter's parish than in any other part of Derby. Of a population which then numbered 3,000, one-third died from the Black Death. One of the symptoms of this plague was a coma or deep sleep. With so many people dying, so many red crosses painted on the doors and bells ringing as the carts rolled through the streets with "Bring out your dead" the common cry, it is hardly surprising that some people, were pronounced dead who were really only in a coma.

St Peter's Church and churchyard, pictured c. 1858 before street widening. There are probably more bodies buried here than in any other Derby church, and naturally, then, more ghostly sightings than most.

Wooden bridge near Ascot Drive, haunted by a headless man, a vampire and accompanied by the smell of rotting fruit.

St Helen's House, Derby's finest surviving Georgian town house, built in 1767 and yet another of the city's buildings said to be haunted by several ghosts.

There are reports at St Peter's of people clawing their way out of shallow graves, or pushing up the lids of coffins and climbing out. So many people died that the town resorted to burying corpses vertically instead of horizontally, but even so they still ran out of space, so many of the unfortunate victims of the Black Death were buried at the boundaries of the town, one of these places still being called Deadman's Lane, off London Road.

There is a reported sighting, at the bottom of Ascot Drive, of a vampire, always accompanied by the smell of rotting fruit. And there is one more vampire tale connected with Derby. The very first public showing, anywhere in the world, of Hamilton Deane's stage adaptation of Bram Stoker's book *Count Dracula* was performed in Derby at the Grand Theatre on 15 May 1924. So Derby theatre audiences were terrified by Dracula before any other in the world.   **R.F.**

St Helen's House

Known affectionately as Pickford's masterpiece and built in 1767, St Helen's House is probably Derby's finest surviving Georgian town house. Built for John Gisbourne of Yoxall Lodge, Staffordshire, in 1767, this fine Palladian mansion once stood in 80 acres of parkland and was visited by society's elite, who would have been almost certainly entertained in some splendour. The house would have had all of the necessary accessories to have impressed the most influential people of the day. Grand balls and dinner parties would have been a regular occurrence at this grand house.

The first monastery in Derbyshire is believed to have existed on the site prior to the present building being erected. In 1137 a man called Tovi gifted a parcel of land to be used as an oratory (chapel) which was dedicated to St Helen and served by a community of Augustinian canons.

St Helen's House has had several

uses in its time including once being owned by William Strutt, eldest son of the industrialist Jedeiah Strutt, who made many improvements to the interior. The building then became Derby School, during which time several new parts were added, including a red- brick chapel.

Today the building is the property of Derbyshire County Council, and houses an adult education centre. There are many who believe that the building would be better utilised as a museum to accommodate some of Derby's treasures including paintings by Joseph Wright, whose pictures quite possibly hung there in earlier days.

Needless to say, the building is said to be haunted by many ghosts. One is said to be that of a young lady, who comes sweeping down the stairs as if hurrying away from something, or someone, that is chasing her. Another ghost is said to be that of a monk who has been seen on several occasions in different parts of the building. One previous lady worker at St Helen's House, who was employed there when it still functioned as a school, informed me that on several occasions whilst she was working late in the evening she had heard an eerie and chilling voice whisper her name. On further investigation this lady found no other person present. When questioning colleagues about her experience she was told that this type of strange occurrence had happened frequently to several people, and some members of staff were so used to this that they had nicknamed the ghost 'The Whisperer'.

Certain parts of the building are also said to have cold spots, and one gentleman, a student at the building in 1992, witnessed a grey smoky figure, seemingly almost of human shape, descend as if from the ceiling and pass through a wall. **W.A.**

The Silk Mill

England's first factory was built here in 1717, on the banks of the River Derwent. John Lombe, who was possibly the world's first industrial spy travelled to Livorno in Italy to steal the patterns for making silk-throwing machines, spending his days working the machines and at night, when he should have been sleeping, copying down their plans. These he carefully placed in bales of silk destined for England. The plans were then intercepted by his father's agents and brought to Derby.

The silk-throwing machines were constructed in Derby's old Guildhall and eventually moved to what was the first purpose-built factory in England. Lombe escaped back home but three years later, so the story goes, he was poisoned by an Italian assassin from Livorno, sent over to this country to exact revenge.

The Silk Mill burnt down in 1910, and all that was saved was the bell tower. It is this tower which is known to be haunted by a little boy who was kicked down the stairs by one of the overseers for not working hard enough.

Children as young as seven were employed at the silk mill. They worked from 5am until 7pm. This little boy's cries can still be heard at

Derby Silk Mill ablaze in 1910. The tower, which was rebuilt, is haunted by the ghost of a small boy.

the foot of the stairs where he bled to death. On many occasions staff of what is now Derby's Industrial Museum have gone into the tower, thinking that there is a child lost, but there is never anyone there. The lift operates by itself, often going up and down on its own. The Silk Mill staff check at night before leaving to make sure that no one is in the lift, as it operates so often in this manner. **R.F.**

Pickford's House Museum

This rather charming property is a Grade I listed building. Built in 1770 by the architect Joseph Pickford as his private town house and work premises, today the building functions as a museum of Georgian life and costume. Other buildings in Friar Gate, including that which houses the publishers of this book, were designed by Pickford, but perhaps his most famous masterpiece in Derby has to be St Helen's House, albeit a sad shadow of its former glorious days when it was first designed and built for John Gisborne in 1767.

The ground floor rooms of Pickford's House are today furnished in a style that might have been used by a Georgian professional man. The upstairs areas of the house, however, are somewhat plain, although I was assured by a curator, when visiting the building, that the upstairs regions of many Georgian properties were normally plain, as professional men such as Pickford would have spent their efforts on decorating and furnishing the ground floor to entertain and to impress visitors and potential clients. Visitors to the museum can see the ground floor rooms furnished in a style close to the original. The kitchen and back kitchen have been reconstructed to a style of the early to mid-19th century, together with a housekeeper's cupboard, cellar, and pantry, giving a feeling of what life might of been like for servants in the last century. At the back of the house a formal Georgian garden has been recreated, making the overall effect of Pickford's House Museum somewhat delightful and charming.

Although there are several ghosts said to haunt the building, the two most prominent ones are that of Pickford's son, who tragically passed away, and a lady seen in the recently recreated kitchens. The death of Joseph Pickford's son apparently had a terrible effect on him and he never completely recovered from his loss. The ghost of the boy has been seen in the front rooms of the building and also in the garden which is also haunted by a gardener who has also often been seen there, dressed in typical Georgian working man's style costume, leaning on his shovel as if having a rest.

Staff working at the building have frequently experienced feelings of 'not being alone' while others claim to have seen the ghosts. Others further maintain that they have actually spoken to the spirits. Pickford's House Museum, however, has a unique atmosphere and a visit to this particularly charming building is strongly recommended, especially as modern surveys of the supernatural show that a ghost is

Pickford's House in Friar Gate. Believed to be haunted by Pickford's son, a former cook and a gardener, all seen wandering the building.

often more likely to be felt rather than seen, and if this is true, then it will be here that such an experience may actually happen. **W.A.**

Friar Gate

Few people who walk up and down Friar Gate ever reflect upon the true meaning of its name which, of course, connects this locality with an ancient religious foundation – the Black Friars. These Dominicans, with the help of King Henry III, built a friary near the site of the present Friary Hotel. In 1329, King Edward II stopped there for refreshments on his way to hunt at Duffield Frith. After the Battle of Shrewsbury, Henry IV lodged there on his royal tour of the land.

The Friary Hotel, scene of several hauntings. The hotel is on the site of a former friary, and also the son of a former owner shot himself dead in the house.

After the Dissolution of the Monasteries by King Henry VIII, the friary became a private house – first being purchased by John Hinde in 1543. The friary passed through several hands before it was eventually demolished. The present building dates from around 1730 and the foundations were laid with stone collected from the original buildings. For some reason the cellars seem incomplete and rather small, and the story goes that when workmen were digging out the cellars for the present building, human remains were disturbed and the decision was made to leave well alone. Thus the Friary Hotel has smaller than average cellars. A map of 1712 clearly shows that the house stands on the part labelled 'Ye Friar close or ye church yard'.

In Victorian times the house was purchased by Henry Mosley, a local printer from the Wardwick. His son was Mayor of Derby in 1847, but in 1857 he shot himself while in the house. Various guests at the hotel have seen a man in Victorian costume walking through the walls of their bedroom. One evening the under manager of the Friary Hotel was drinking with customers at the bar when they saw a headless figure dressed in a black robe disappear through the panelling of the room. A few minutes later they were badly jostled against the bar, each looking at the other and asking, "Did you do that?" No one would own up to it.

A former waiter at the Friary Hotel claimed that he once met a black friar in one of the basement corridors and the apparition vanished through a wall. This waiter had never believed in ghosts until that moment and, strangely enough, had worked at the Lady in Grey restaurant at Shardlow, another very haunted building, but had never seen any ghostly apparitions in that building. His first encounter was at the Friary Hotel in Derby.   **R.F.**

Jacobean House

This was Derby's first brick building, built in 1611. It was once much larger, having five gables until in 1855 when the Victorians drove Becket Street right through the house. Mrs Gisbourne, the wife of Derby's mayor, was the first lady within the town to have her own coach. When she left her home her servants and retainers accompanied her to the borders of Derbyshire, either to help her negotiate the foul, deep-rutted roads of the time, or perhaps to make sure that she was really gone! To this day, a mysterious phantom coach and horses are sometimes seen parked

The Jacobean House is one of Derby's most haunted buildings. A solicitor who worked there had to move because of could no longer stand the hauntings.

outside the house and a headless coachman has been seen coming through the coach archway which may still be seen on the left-hand side of the building. Also, the dark, mysterious figure of a man is seen standing in the Wardwick entrance to the house. A solicitor who once had offices in the building, moved his premises elsewhere as he could no longer stand working in the building late at night, due to the strange things that happened there when he was alone.

Wayne Anthony in his book *Derbyshire Ghosts*, (J.H.Hall & Sons, 1992) describes how one lady, Mrs Hall, a former worker at the building experienced the following: "I was in the upstairs rooms of Jacobean House, looking for something or other, when I felt someone brush past me and immediately turning, I caught sight of a lady in a blue dress,

The Jacobean House showing all five gables before Becket Street was built.

who turned her head to look at me, smiled and walked down the stairs. I immediately followed her, and on reaching the bottom floor I asked colleagues if they had seen anyone pass them, to which they replied that no one had, as far as they were aware. I left it at that and did not tell them why I had asked such a strange question. Later on that week, I saw the lady again, this time going up the stairs, and still wearing the same blue

Looking from Friar Gate to the Wardwick with the Jacobean House on the right. This area of Derby has been the scene of several hauntings.

dress, the only difference being that she had added a white shawl which hung loosely around her shoulders.

"Again I followed her. On reaching the upper floors of the building, I could find no trace of the woman. Shortly after this event had taken place, work colleagues came rushing into the room where I was working and stated that they had just seen the ghost of a lady in blue walking up the stairs, who had vanished before their eyes. It was at this point that others working in the room stated they too had experienced similar visitations. I saw her many times during my employment within the building, always in blue and always in the vicinity of the stairs, I was never frightened of meeting her and in many ways I looked forward to seeing her, for she always looked so gentle and kind and I don't think that she would ever hurt anyone. Whenever anything went missing – and things very often did – we always put it down to the 'Blue Lady' moving them. Some things were never found and some things would turn up days or weeks later, but never when they were needed."

There are a reported 14 ghosts in Jacobean House, making the building one of the most haunted within the city of Derby.   **R.F.**

Derby Assembly Rooms

As in other towns, the Assembly Rooms in Derby was a popular meeting place in the 18th century, where young people danced and the elderly people played cards whilst keeping a watchful eye on their offspring. The aim of an assembly

46

was to bring all sorts and classes of people together harmoniously, but in Derby this was not to be, certainly not around 1714 as there had evolved two very separate assemblies: one at the corner of the Market Place and Full Street for the gentry of the county and one for the lesser

The concourse at the new Derby Assembly Rooms. The manager and another member of staff saw the ghost of a woman in this area.

mortals of the town. This second assembly was situated at Moote Hall or meeting place, part of which still exists, although now incorporated into the modern facade of the Derbyshire Building Society on the corner of the Market Place and Iron Gate.

A bizarre incident happened there on the night of 5 December 1745. People had come from far and wide to a reception held there for Prince Charles Edward Stuart, who had arrived in Derby on his way to take the English crown. The crush of people was so great that a table bearing the Royal Standard was overturned and the standard was broken. This was considered a bad omen by many of the prince's army and, although the decision was taken on military grounds alone, following that fateful reception the order was given for the retreat of the Highland army back north. There eventually followed, of course, the Battle of Culloden, the slaughter and transportation of hundreds of Scots, the burning of their homes, the killing of their cattle and eventually, the Highland Clearances.

A county assembly had been built in Derby in 1714, and an even larger building was erected on the Market Place in 1763. This was badly damaged by fire 200 years later and a much larger Assembly Rooms, opened in 1977, now occupies the old site on the Market Place, including the site of the Duke of Newcastle's house, where King Charles I stayed in 1637. The modern Assembly Rooms complex still provides entertainment for Derbyshire people as well as playing host to national exhibitions and sporting events.

According to many people, the present building is haunted. Mick Taylor, the house manager, was in the building at 3am one morning, standing in the concourse with his back to the Darwin Suite. Also present was another member of staff. Mr Taylor turned around – why, he did not know – and saw an elderly lady dressed in Victorian costume. She appeared to have no legs and seemed to be floating. He alerted his colleague, who also turned around, and both witnessed the figure gliding across the floor before disappearing.

On many other occasions, security guards have seen what appeared to be a ring of children dancing in the Darwin Suite and have often reported the eerie sounds of laughter when there is no one in the building.

The new Assembly Rooms were

built between 1973 and 1977. As the footings and foundations were being installed a builder reported seeing what he believed, along with several work colleagues, to be the remains of an old Viking ship, and of course this is quite feasible as the site is close to the River Derwent. He reported the matter to his superiors but was told that because of a penalty clause in the contract, the work had to be finished on time and so hundreds of tons of concrete were poured over the remains of what might have proved to be one of Derby's most important links with the past. **R.F.**

Normanton Barracks

For more than a century the red brick buildings and tall tower of Normanton Barracks, home of the Sherwood Foresters, were a major feature of the area at the top of Sinfin Lane. Indeed, even today Derbeians still refer to 'the Barracks' as a location, even though the last soldiers left there more than 30 years ago.

Nothing now remains of the original buildings which were erected in 1876 and which closed their gates for the final time in 1963, later being acquired by the Department of Transport for a road scheme which was eventually shelved. The land remained largely unused, although some small business units were to function there for some years to come and the local council used part of the site as a recreation centre.

Eventually the land was sold and redeveloped for its present use with a multi-screen cinema, bowling alley, small hotel and restaurant, fast-food outlets and a bingo club.

Shortly after the Barracks was closed, reports began to surface concerning ghostly apparitions which had been seen in the area of the tower and main buildings. According to local legend, a phantom coach, complete with driver and horses, haunts the area and is often seen on moonlit nights being pulled by two headless horses. The ghosts are said to be the result of a tragic accident which happened when a tannery occupied part of the site. It is said that the coach and horses fell into a cesspit which swallowed up the driver, carriage and his animals. They were never recovered and local youngsters were often warned about playing on the site of this apparently 'bottomless' pit..

Several of the workers involved in building the present development related to me accounts of strange happenings there. One man, working late at night, had on several occasions thought that he had heard his name being called even though no one else was in the building. The same man had also experienced sudden blasts of cold air which made his hair stand on end, and although he had never seen anything 'not of this world', he was quite convinced that the building was indeed haunted.

One lady, Miss Jacqueline O'Connell, informed me that on several occasions, whilst working under contract at several of the premises, she had seen the ghost of a man in a soldier's uniform sitting watching her. On one occasion she was cleaning in a part of the building

The main gate of Normanton Barracks pictured around World War One. Although the area is now unrecognisable, ghosts are still said to haunt the site including that of a young soldier.

alleged to be haunted when she noticed a boot in one of the aisles. Thinking it odd that someone should leave such an item, she stepped over it and continued with cleaning the carpets. When she turned around to pick up the boot, it was gone and she is convinced that it was that of the ghostly soldier who she described as having dark hair, and being no older than his mid-30s with a pleasant face.

On another occasion she heard strange rustling noises and turned around to find the ghost of an old lady, dressed in an old fashioned way, looking at her and smiling. Eventually Jacqueline 'knew' when the lady was going to appear, as the smell of flowers pervaded the atmosphere shortly before an appearance. In one part of the building there was apparently an area which was always very cold, even though heaters were on, day and night.

Several people apparently resigned because of the hauntings and many workers said they felt that they were being constantly watched. Others, like Jacqueline O'Connell, claimed that they knew when ghosts were present because of a strange sweet smell. **W.A.**

The Grand Theatre Ghosts

The Grand Theatre in Derby was the innovation of Andrew Melville, who was waiting for a train on Derby Midland Station, wandered into the town, saw a plot of land available on

The Grand Theatre, Babington Lane. The world's first stage adaptation of Dracula was put on here but by then the building already had spooky connections. The first theatre burned down and two men, an actor and a carpenter, who died in the fire are said to haunt the Grand, which is now the Eclipse night spot.

Babington Lane and decided to build himself a theatre. The Grand Theatre opened on 25 March 1886. Only two months later, on 3 May, Edward Terry and his comedy company opened in the town. Melville expected the comedy to draw a good house in Derby, so at 6.45pm on that Thursday night, he was sitting in the stalls with his secretary along with 30 patrons.

A noise was heard coming from the back stage, indicating that something was wrong. Quietly, Melville slipped through the pass door to find out what was the matter. When he arrived back stage, he noticed that one of the borders was alight, presumably caused by it coming into contact with a gas jet. The border was cut down and crashed into the stage, but by now other scenery in the flys had also caught fire. The felled border was also setting fire to the stage in several places. Melville quickly sent a messenger for the fire brigade and put his head through the axe drop to warn the audience that something was wrong and that they should leave

the theatre as quickly and as quietly as possible. He then showed members of Terry's company the way out, before returning to make sure that the audience had left. Melville left the theatre to check that the fire brigade was on the way.

The stage by now was well ablaze – the fire hydrants were not working properly – and volumes of smoke were rising from the stage. It was then discovered that not everyone had escaped. The unconscious body of the 24-year-old actor, John Adams, was dragged clear of the conflagration by William Hill and conveyed to the Infirmary in a butcher's cart. Alas, Adams died on the way.

In the early hours of Friday morning, news filtered through that James Locksley, a carpenter employed at the theatre, had not returned to his East Derwent Street lodgings, and a search of the burnt-out theatre revealed his charred corpse near the stage door.

The extent of the damage to the Grand Theatre was estimated at £10,000 but, regardless, Andrew Melville promised to rebuild his theatre. The moralists, of course, had a field day, naturally believing that the fire had been the judgement of the Almighty which they had anticipated would, in time, be pronounced. On the Saturday night following the fire one religious enthusiast got up in Derby Market Place and expressed his satisfaction at the burning of the theatre. His only regret was that more of the disreputable people who frequented such places were not burned with it! Within six months of the fire, on

Saturday 13 November, Derby's Grand Theatre reopened.

The building, in recent years having undergone several reincarnations as a night spot, is allegedly haunted. Apparently few people will go up into 'the gods' alone, feeling another presence there; and a figure has often been seen on the main staircase. Perhaps it is the young actor who died so tragically on the night of Thursday, 6 May 1886. **R.F.**

Elvaston Castle and Churchyard

Elvaston Castle, which is five miles south-east of Derby, has been a country park since 1970. Four centuries earlier it belonged to the Earls of Harrington. The present building is on the site of a much older house, which dated from the 16th century.

A bay window from the earlier house is incorporated into the present building and it is from this window that the figure of a lady in

Elvaston Castle, Cromwell's troops, a ghostly white lady and a phantom dog have been experienced here.

white has been seen moving from side to side as if sitting in a rocking chair. She is also frequently observed going from the house into the nearby churchyard. One worker at the castle told me that the figure is regularly heard going from room to room, banging doors and generally making a nuisance of herself. She has also been seen wandering the churchyard looking at gravestones and muttering to herself.

No one seems to know whether the 'White Lady' originates from the castle or the church. The church dates back to the 13th century, although another possibly existed there before the present one was built. Many people have seen her accompanied by a large white dog not unlike a Wolf Hound, in the grounds of the castle. Local legend says that she was a daughter of an earl, who died of a broken heart because her betrothed had been killed during some war.

One other interesting story concerning Elvaston Castle comes from a Mr Peter Flower, an extremely down-to-earth former military man, not given to flights of the imagination, who recounted to me the following story: "Whilst living at Elvaston many years ago, namely just off Elvaston Lane, which now leads through Raynesway and on through to St Michael's Church and then to Elvaston Castle, in the early hours – around 2.00 a.m – of a summer's morning I heard what sounded like a troop of horsemen cantering down the lane. Apart from the noise of hooves there was the sound of the usual trappings of military type horsemen – harness, swords etc. I saw nothing but I did make enquiries of some of the older residents in the area, and they confirmed that these noises had been heard before, and that local legend had it that they were the ghosts of a troop of Oliver Cromwell's men on their way to El-vaston Castle. On reflection, the year that I experienced this phenomenon would have been 1960." **W.A.**

Swarkestone Bridge

Swarkestone Bridge is almost a mile in length and crosses an area of low-lying marshy land as well as the River Trent. It was originally built in the early 13th century, on behalf of two beautiful sisters of the Bellamont family, in memory of their fiancés, as legend has it.

The sisters were holding a party to celebrate their joint betrothal when the two young men were summoned to attend a meeting of barons on the other side of the Trent. They reached the meeting safely, but while they were there, the river became swollen by a rainstorm. Although it became a flood of rushing water, the men were eager to get back to their beautiful sweethearts and attempted to ford the river on horseback. Their horses swam valiantly against the torrent but their efforts were in vain. Both men were swept away and drowned.

The heartbroken Bellamont girls built the bridge over the Trent to pre-vent such a tragedy occurring again, and in memory of the drowned men. Neither girl ever married. In fact the legend states that they spent so much money on the bridge that they died not only unwed, but also in extreme poverty, being buried in one grave in Prestwold Church in Leicestershire. Their ghosts are said to be seen on stormy nights when the River Trent is swollen, looking for their lost loves who were so tragically drowned in the river's murky waters.

When Charles Edward Stuart and his small army of Highlanders reached Derby on 4 December 1745, one of their most important tasks was to send a party the seven miles from Derby to Swarkestone to try to secure the bridge over the River Trent. Swarkestone Bridge is the longest stone bridge in England, and in 1745 it was the only bridge across the River Trent between Burton and Nottingham. For the prince's army it was also the only way to London and probable victory.

Seventy Highland soldiers, prob-ably cavalry, were sent to secure the bridge, and they reached it four hours before Government troops, who had been ordered to destroy the bridge to stop Charlie's army from crossing it. Those 70 Scottish soldiers held Swarkestone Bridge until 6 December. Some of them went over it to Melbourne, to warn locals to prepare billets for the Highland army when they crossed over on their way to take the throne from King George II. This was not to be, of course, the decision being made at Derby to turn back. Thus, Swarkestone Bridge was the farthest point south reached by Bonnie Prince Charlie's troops.

Swarkestone Bridge, where the ghostly sounds of soldiers have been hard. Is it the sound of phantom Cavaliers, or of Bonnie Prince Charlie's advance party?

Some 102 years earlier there had been a skirmish on Swarkestone Bridge between troops of Bonnie Prince Charlie's great-grandfather, Charles I, and those of Oliver Cromwell during the English Civil War. Sir John Harpur of Swarkestone fortified his own home, and the bridge as well. Sir John Gell, the Parliamentary commandant of Derby, led his own regiment out of the town and hurled them against the Royalist barricades at Swarkestone Bridge. Seven or eight men were killed during that skirmish.

There have been many strange sightings at Swarkestone, one of the most interesting coming from a gentleman who told me: "I was walking my dog. It was late at night and it had just started to rain when in the distance, I could hear the sound of horses' hooves. I thought at the time that it was locals out for a late ride. This thought was soon dismissed as the noise of horses' hooves became accompanied by the sound of clatter and talking which became louder and louder. My curiosity aroused, I waited in anticipation for the late riders to appear. They never did, although the noises became louder still, until, in

the end when I thought that I could take it no more, the noise and the chaotic clatter stopped.

"My dog Harvey, with me all the time that the clamour was taking place, seemed not to have been affected by what had happened. Further along Swarkestone Bridge, I met a lady who also was walking her dogs and asked her if she had seen or heard anything. She looked at me blankly, stating that she did not know what I was talking about. I also asked two other people in the vicinity but they, likewise, denied hearing anything. Several months later, I was telling an elderly aunt about my experience. She did not seem unduly surprised and when I had finished she told me that she too had heard something similar in 1948. My aunt also told me that what I had experienced was apparently the ghosts of Bonnie Prince Charlie and his Highlanders trying to cross the bridge."

Is it possible that this gentleman heard the ghosts of a cavalry detachment belonging to Bonnie Prince Charlie as they were being recalled back to Derby for the long retreat to Scotland and the eventual destruction of the Highland army at the Battle of Culloden? Or could of been the battling troops of Charles I and Cromwell's armies re-enacting a skirmish on Swarkestone Bridge on 5 January 1643?   **W.A. & .R.F.**

Mackworth Castle

What we see of Mackworth Castle today is said to be a gatehouse which

Mackworth Castle, haunted by several ghosts including a phantom horse rider heard galloping down the lane.

was probably built some time at the beginning of the 15th century. There is much debate as to whether a castle existed, on or near the site, although a large keep platform has at one time been excavated. It is believed by many that the castle was destroyed by Parliamentary forces during the English Civil War, but if this were so there would surely be a certain amount of scars to be found on the gateway.

The castle that never was, as it is often locally referred to, still causes much debate amongst local historians. Was there a great castle at Mackworth? Is what we see simply a folly? No one really knows for sure, although it would per-haps be safe to assume that a great castle was indeed intended for the site before a change of mind meant that the structure never actually came into being.

Two ghosts are said to haunt the site around the gatehouse. One is said to be that of a man dressed in green, the other an old lady who is said to be bent over and very old. Dressed in a white apron, she just smiles and then fades away. One other strange phen-omenon reported about the site is that, on certain days of the year, a strange mist has been seen moving through the gates. A local to the area informed me that he had often heard the sound of a single horse's hooves coming along the lane near the gatehouse. He described the sound as, 'fast and furious', as if whoever it might be was in a hurry to get to where they were going.　　**W.A.**

Holy Ghosts

Joan Waste

Born over 400 years ago to a poor barber and rope maker who lived in the parish of All Hallows, Derby, was a blind girl who was to become known as the Derby Martyr. From an early age Joan Waste, daughter of William Waste, was obviously a determined child, for although she lived in a world of darkness she could do most things that sighted people could do, including knitting and darning, and she was also proficient in making hose and sleeves for doublets. Joan also occasionally worked alongside her father and became quite adept at making rope.

She was very close to her family and when her mother and father died she went to live with her twin brother, Roger, to whom she was very close and who had helped her a great deal as the twins grew up. By this time she had already developed a strong religious leaning and would attend church on a daily basis, very rarely missing a service. It is said that her devotion to religion was so great that she could find her way to all the churches in Derby unaccompanied, which was undoubtedly an accomplishment for someone with such a disability.

Struggling against adversity was nothing new to Joan and when she decided that she wanted to do something there seemed to be very little that could stop her. She was so determined to buy a *Holy Bible* that she went without many things before saving enough money to purchase a copy of the *New Testament*.

Like many blind people, Joan Waste was gifted with an excellent memory and would commit to mind most of what she heard about religion and theology. In time she became friendly with a man called John Hurt, who was serving a prison sentence for debt. Joan would often visit Hurt in prison and he would read passages from the Bible to her, passages which Joan would commit to memory. When he was not able to read to her, she would enlist the help of the local clerk to the parish of All Saints', a man by the name of John Pemerton. She was also known to pay a penny or two for the assistance of other people. Before long her knowledge of the *Holy Bible* was apparently astounding.

When King Edward VI died and his sister Mary ascended the throne, England was thrown into religious turmoil as the religious reforms introduced by the king were abolished and the religious doctrine of the pre-Reformation period were restored. England was thrown into panic and hundreds of people were imprisoned for their religious beliefs.

Joan Waste was one of them and was taken to gaol and interrogated by an official called Peter Finch. She denied the doctrine of transubstantiation, a stance which was construed as heresy and resulted in her being summoned before the Bishop of the diocese, Rafe Baine, his chancellor Sir John Port, Peter Finch, William Bainbridge and several others who accordingly charged Joan Waste with the following:

'First, that she did holde the sacrament of the alter, to be but onlie a memorie or representation of Christe's bodie, and materiall bread and wine, but not his naturall bodie unless it were received, as that it ought not to be reserved from time to time over the alter, but immediatelie to be received, &c.

"Item, That she did holde, in receiving of the sacrament of the alter, she did not receive the same body that was borne of the Virgin Mary, and suffered upon the crosse for our redemption, &c.

"Item, She did holde, that Christ at his last supper, did not blesse the bread that he had then in his handes, but was blessed himself, and by virtue of his wordes of consecration, the substance of the bread and wine is not converted and turned into the substance of the bodie and blood of Christ.

"Item, She did graunt that she was of the parish of Alhalowes, in Darbie, &c.

"Item, That all and singular the premises are true and notorious by publicke report and fame, &c."

Joan Waste then told the learned gathering that her beliefs were founded upon the Holy Scripture and the teachings other learned men, many of whom were suffering imprisonment and death rather than denounce their beliefs and take up with the new doctrine.

She then went on to mention a certain Dr Taylor, who had died for his beliefs, and she then said to her examiners that, 'if they would doe so in like case for their doctrine, which if they would not, she desired them, for God's sake, not to trouble her, being a blinde, poore and unlearned woman, with any further talke, saying (by God's assistance) that she was readie to yeeld up her life in that faith, in such sort as they should appoint'.

Further discussions continued and it soon became obvious that Joan Waste was not going to alter her beliefs. In a further attempt to change the girl's mind, the gathering resorted to threats of torture, imprisonment and death. This seemed to have the desired effect and she told the bishop, Rafe Baine, if he would, 'take it upon his conscience, that the doctrine which he would have her believe concerning the sacrament was true, and that at the dreadful day of judgment he would answer for her therein, she would then further answer them'.

The bishop seems to be about to agree with Joan when, Sir John Port interrupted their conversation and pointed out: "My lord you know not what you do; you may in no case answer for an heretic." Sir John Port asked Joan if she would abjure all that she believed concerning her doctrine of beliefs. This she refused to do, stating that if the bishop would not accept responsibility for what they would have her believe, then she would thank them to trouble her no more, and do with her what they saw fit.

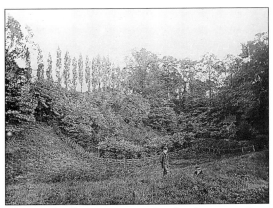

The Windmill Pit on Burton Road, where poor Joan Waste was burned at the stake. Her ghost haunts the area. Or is it the ghost of a murderess who also met this grisly fate?

Following this statement she was imprisoned for several weeks, in which time it was no doubt hoped that she would recant.

It is hard to imagine what this poor blind girl must have been thinking, especially in the time that she was imprisoned awaiting a written *De hacretico coinubrindo*. It finally arrived and Joan Waste was taken to All Saints' Church, where her accusers, no doubt with grim faces awaited her. When she arrived she was led to the front of the pulpit where Dr Draicott gave an incriminating sermon and accused her of denying the doctrine of transubstantiation and told her that she was not only physically, but spiritually blind. He told her that the fire that was going to consume her mortal flesh would also consume her soul, leaving her spiritually void for eternity.

Further accusations followed but still stronger must have been Joan's faith in the doctrine that she had come to believe in, for she would not relent and held firmly to her faith,

even towards her last moments when she 'cried unto Christ to have mercy upon her as long as life served'.

It was no doubt a pathetic scene on 1 August, 1556, as Joan Waste was led to the scene of her execution, clutching the hand of her beloved twin brother Roger. Who knows what words of solace were spoken between the two, and when the flames seared her flesh, Joan, the poor blind girl, aged but 22 years, was to enter the pages of Derby's history.

Some say the place where Joan Waste was burned at the stake to be 'accursed ground'. Others believe that the ghost of the poor blind girl still haunts the spot, whilst there are equally as many people who believe that the history of this notorious execution spot is far darker and sinister than many historians would have us believe. It is a fact that people were burnt at the stake at Windmill Pit, now near Lime Avenue off Burton Road, and although there is little proof, it is equally quite likely that witches and those accused of practising the 'dark arts', were burnt to their deaths at this historically sinister spot when frenzied religious persecution ravaged the land.

Many people living near here believe that strange things can often be seen in the area, if one is so inclined to observe. However, most people in the vicinity say that they are quite happy to do so as they find the accommodation of most of the houses to be with character and quite pleasing.

The last person to be burned at the stake in this area was a woman found guilty of poisoning her husband in

1601. It is thought by many that the residential ghost of the area is actually this murderess rather than the unsettled spirit of the devoutly religious Joan Waste.   **W.A.**

St Alkmund's Well

Alkmund was the son of King Alcred of Northumbria. In 774AD Alkmund was forced to flee with his father in order to evade their rebellious subjects who had mostly joined forces with the conquering Danes. For 20 years Alkmund and his father lived amongst the Picts. Learning much from them he soon came to realise that riches and luxury were not what he craved from life; instead he chose to help his people regain their lands, putting himself at the head of his armies and fighting for what he believed to be his.

There is much debate as to how Alkmund lost his life. Some scholars would have it that he was slain in the battle of Kempsford in the year 800AD, others that he was killed by Prince Ardulph in the same year, while others still strongly maintain

St Alkmund's Well, near to where a ghostly monk has been seen.

that he was more likely to have met his end at the hands of the Danes in the year 819AD, although Butler is of a slightly differing opinion in *Lives of the Saints, Vol II:*

'During his temporal prosperity, the greater he was in power so much the more meek and humble was he in his heart, and so much the more affable to others. He was poor amidst riches, because he knew no greater pleasure than to strip himself for the relief of the distressed. Being driven from his kingdom, together with his father, by rebellious subjects in league with Danish plunderers, he lived among the Picts above 20 years in banishment; learning more heartily to despise earthly vanities, and making it his whole study to serve the King of kings. His subjects groaning under the yoke of an unsupportable tyranny, took up arms against their oppressors, and induced the royal prince, upon motives of compassion for their distress and a holy zeal for religion, to put himself at their head. Several battles were prosperously fought; but at length the pious prince was murdered by the contrivance of King Eardulf."

Shortly after his death, Alkmund was made a saint and martyr. He was buried at Lilleshall, in Shropshire, within a church that already existed or else within a church that was built especially to house his remains. His body was not to stay at Lilleshall for very long, however, as it was greatly feared that the Danes would try to destroy it or take it perhaps for ransom. His remains therefore were hastily removed and transferred to Northworthy, the embryonic Derby,

The site of the first St Alkmund's Church, now demolished.

Artist's impression of St Alkmund's Church in 1844. The church was later demolished to make way for a road development but the site is said to be haunted by several ghosts.

for safe keeping. According to legend St Alkmund's remains rested for a short while near a well. Thereafter the water from the well was said to have miraculous healing powers. Mr Cantrell, the vicar of the first St Alkmund's Church (now long since demolished) writing to a Dr Pegg on the subject in 1760 said: 'Fuller in his 'Worthies' reports of miracles here. I add that it has been commonly said here that the north countrymen inquire for this tomb and rest their packs upon it'. Also mentioned in the letter was a reference to the miraculous healing qualities that the water had on the vicar of St Werburgh's (Revd William Locket), who 'being of low consumption' took to drinking the water on a daily basis and recovered his health.

The well, known as St Alkmund's Well, exists today and is said to be haunted by a monk, who is seen wandering around the vicinity dressed in a dark brown habit. One gentleman, having lived in the area for over 30 years was familiar with the story of the ghostly monk and assured me that he had seen this strange figure on several occasions, not just in the vicinity of the well but also on and near Darley Playing Fields.

Indeed, the whole area is said to be haunted including several flats nearby where one lady occupant informed me that she had been constantly plagued by mysterious knocking noises. Several times this lady, whom I shall refer to as Janet, had thought that pranksters were deliberately knocking on her door. One night, Janet told me, about 7pm, when the knocking noises seemed to be at their most active, she waited and on the first knock, – there were normally three in loud slow succession – she pulled open the door quickly, only to find nobody there. As time passed Janet found that the knocking noises were not confined to her front door. Several times she was disturbed from her sleep by knocking sounds coming from within her bedroom, although each time investigations revealed nothing. On questioning some of her neighbours Janet found that several of them had also experienced the strange knocking noises. Even now, five years later, Janet still hears the knocking noises

Dr C.A.R.Radford examines the sarcophagus discovered under St Alkmund's when the church was demolished in the late 1960s. At one time it was thought to have contained the remains of Alkmund himself.

The several stages of the excavation of the sarcophagus found under St Alkmund's.

Further stages of the excavation under St Alkmund's.

although not nearly as frequent as they used to be and she thinks that she has perhaps become accustomed to them.

Janet was familiar with the story of St Alkmund's Well and thinks that the phantom knocking could be somehow connected with the legend of the healing well.

Phantom knocking noises are not uncommon, even though most ghost books do not mention them. These strange tappings, referred to as 'Knockers' have been recorded throughout history, especially in the South of England. Derbyshire also has its fare share of these troublesome spirits, where they are found most commonly in lead mines. Legend states that the phantom knockers are the ghosts of Jews who took part in the Crucifixion and were sent to England, especially Cornwall, to work in the mines as punishment. It is said that miners will not mark anything with the sign of the cross for fear of annoying them. It is a fact that Jews did work in the mines of Cornwall in the 11th and 12th centuries, thereby giving some credence to the belief in these ghosts. As previously mentioned several mines in Derbyshire are said to be haunted by these knocking spirits, which are believed to be omens of bad luck. **W.A.**

Some one came knocking At my wee, small door;
Some one came knocking,
I'm sure-sure-sure;
I listened, I opened,
I looked to left and right, But nought there was a-stirring
In the still dark night; Only the busy beetle
Tap-tapping in the wall,
Only from the forest
The screech-owl's call,
Only the cricket whistling
While the dewdrops fall, So I know not who came knocking,
At all, at all, at all.

Walter De La Mare (1873-1956)

Derby Cathedral

The rapid increase in the population of England in the late 19th and early 20th century resulted in the creation of new bishoprics and several hitherto 'ordinary' churches becoming cathedrals. There was neither the time nor the money to build the sort of grand new cathedrals which had risen in Norman times, and new bishops were designated existing churches as their seats. Thus, in 1927 All Saints' Church in Derby became Derby Cathedral.

Thought to have been founded by King Edmund in 943AD, All Saints' has been altered considerably over the centuries. At the beginning of the 18th century, the only thing that could have been said to have been striking about this church was its tower, 212ft tall – the second highest parish church tower in England – and built in the time of Henry VIII.

In 1723 the church was deemed unsafe and it seems that no one was prepared to do anything about it until a particularly courageous churchman, Revd Dr Michael Hutchinson, ordered that the entire structure – except the tower – should be demolished. The decision was unpopular with local people but shortly afterwards plans for the rebuilding were submitted by James Gibbs, who became famous for many of his churches including St Mary-le-Strand and perhaps his most famous work, St Martin-in-the Fields, in London. The designs for a new All Saints' were accepted and work soon began, resulting in the magnificent church which we know today as Derby Cathedral.

Working in association with Gibbs was Robert Bakewell, an ironsmith whose striking wrought-iron screen remains one of the most notable features of the Cathedral's interior. Other notable features include the remarkable baldachino; several memorial carvings, many to notable Derbyshire families, one of which is Bess of Hardwick's monument which was built and completed within her own lifetime.

Another interesting memorial is a

The ghosts of a white lady and of John Crossland, a Derby hangman, have been seen near Derby Cathedral.

Several ghosts are said to haunt the vicinity of Derby Cathedral including that of Charles Edward Stuart, seen by a lady who lived in a building, now a shop, across the road. She told me her story of how she often sees a man in Jacobite dress walk into the Cathedral: "On many occasions I had seen the vague ghostly shape of a man in Jacobite costume walking near the Cathedral. Being familiar with the story of Bonnie Prince Charlie and his visit to Derby I presumed that it was the prince recounting his footsteps, perhaps trying to understand how it had all gone wrong for him. My mother once saw this figure and she too was convinced that it had been the ghost of Bonnie Prince Charlie."

It is interesting to note that a ghostly figure in 'Cavalier' style dress has also been spotted not too far from this spot at the Silk Mill public house.

Many other ghosts have been seen about Derby Cathedral including a 'white lady' seen walking down the steps at the back of the church, a young woman seen crying and a small boy. Also said to wander the grounds is the unhappy ghost of John Crossland, a former executioner, originally himself a criminal, who was granted a pardon on the under-

tablet on the south wall near the steps to St Katherine's Chapel, which commemorates an historic visit from Prince Charles Edward Stuart, who visited All Saints' in December 1745. The Young Pretender had marched with his army virtually unchallenged from Carlisle. On reaching Derby his troops were stationed about the town and the prince is said to have ordered the bells of All Saints' to be rung and, with his officers accompanying him, he attended a service at the church.

The Cavendish Vault and St Katherine's Chapel in Derby Cathedral, prior to the vault being sealed off in 1973. The coffins pictured here contain the remains of members of the Cavendish family.

Bonnie Prince Charlie – this is a memorial tablet in Derby Cathedral – is alleged to haunt the place his quest for the crown of England was abandoned.

Many ghosts have been seen about Derby Cathedral including a 'white lady' seen walking down the steps at the back of the church, a young woman seen crying and the phantom of a small boy. Also said to wander the grounds is the unhappy ghost of John Crossland, a former executioner who hanged his own father and brother. In the distance at left can be seen 46 Queen Street (see also page 94).

standing that he become the executioner for the sentence of death passed on his father and brother. This he agreed to do and from then on became the busiest executioner in the county, frequently being used by several other shires. His ghost is said to be seen often wandering the grounds, at the side of the Cathedral, seeking to find peace for his tormented and guilty soul. **W.A.**

Haunted Monastries

A small priory, with a hospital attached, dedicated to St James once stood near the corner of St James's Lane (now the present St James's Street). The order consisted of Cluniac monks who originated from Cluny in France. The main focus of their order was the emphasis on daily worship and prayer while manual labour and normal daily routine was left to paid servants. Eventually over 35 Cluniac houses were established in England, the vast majority of them being small establishments housing rarely more than three to four monks.

An influential Derby man named Waltheof Fitsueni gifted the church of St James to the Cluniac priory of Bermondsey in 1140, which was ruled over by a prior from their own community.

The St James's priory was a relatively poor one and rarely exceeded an annual income of more than £5 from the lands which it held. Additional income came from a toll which the monks operated across St James's Bridge which spanned Markeaton Brook and linking St James's Lane with the Wardwick. In 1279 the house consisted of a prior and two monks. Around the same time one monk was found to be living 'disreputably'. The disgraced monk was sent to do penance in Bermondsey whilst another monk was dispatched to Derby to take his place.

Disaster struck in the 14th century when the priory, church and hospital were destroyed by fire. The priory is thought to have been almost certainly constructed of wood and therefore the

Derby's Cornmarket pictured in the latter half of the 19th century and showing a broader view of the area which once housed a small priory. St James's Lane can be seen on the right (note the two supporting girders across the lane). The bridge over Markeaton Brook, for which the monks collected tolls, was at the other end of the lane. Opposite was the Lock-Up and the area under which the ghost of a small boy was seen.

A small priory, with a hospital attached, dedicated to St James, once stood near this corner of St James's Lane, now St James's Street.

rebuilding of it should have been accomplished in a relatively short time.

Royal protection had been given to various religious orders under Edward II which, at that time, enabled the prior and his monks to collect alms. The rebuilt small priory and hospital survived until the Dissolution of the Monasteries in 1536, after which very little is known about the priory.

Present-day St James's Street is a busy commercial thoroughfare and one would hardly notice the St James' Hotel, near the junction with the Cornmarket if one was not already aware of its existence, so well does it blend in with the surrounding shops and office premises.

The ghost of a monk has frequently been seen in this vicinity and there are also many reports from surrounding shops and offices of strange noises and phantom footsteps that have been heard from time to time. The former hotel – the establishment is now simply another town centre public house, known to one and all as 'Jimmy's' – is said to be haunted by a previous worker and the lift has been known to move between floors of its own accord. One cleaning lady, who used to work in several of the buildings which now occupy the site of the previous priory, told me that she had 'often heard the sound of singing'. The reader may be tempted to say, "Well, it is a pub!" but according to the lady the noise 'sounded more like monks chanting'. Not too far from this spot is where the ghost of a young boy was seen in a tunnel beneath the foundations of the

old William & Glyn's Bank, near the Lock-Up Yard.

Other monasteries and religious houses in the Derby area are also said to be haunted by ghostly monks and nuns. Disembodied hands and strange moaning noises have been experienced at the Friary Hotel which stands near the site of the original friary which was established around the year 1230 and belonged to the Dominicans or Blackfriars who had arrived in England around 1221. The Blackfriars soon established themselves in Derby and acquired some land just outside the boundary of the medieval town, close to Bramble Brook near Uttoxeter Road.

Another ghost story connected with the area concerns a young man who was awakened in the night while staying at lodgings in a boarding house which overlooked the Friary Hotel car-park. According to him he had retired to bed and awoke in the early hours of the morning to find a nun walking around his room ringing a small bell. So frightened was the young man that the very next day he packed his bags and left. Whilst preparations for a car-park were taking place at the back of the hotel, bones of what was believed to be a friar were unearthed.

Shortly after these remains were found, strange garbed figures and ghostly nuns were sighted near here. One lady, Carol, a local worker to the area, informed me that beneath her place of work is a cellar which, according to local legend, is one of the alleged secret passages that run hither and thither beneath the streets of the Friar Gate area and beyond. She recounted to me a time when she had taken some boxes of excess equipment down to the cellars for storage. On entering the cellar she had seen the strange figure of what appeared to be a monk, in a brown habit, which appeared to be hovering a foot or so above the floor level. So frightened was Carol by what she saw that she threw what she was carrying to the floor and ran back upstairs to alert another office manager.

The manager, David, immediately went back down to the basement to investigate, thinking that perhaps a vagrant or a thief must have somehow managed to sneak past them. On reaching the basement there appeared to be no one in the room. However, as David retraced his steps, back up the cellar stairs, he was shocked to see what appeared to be a disembodied pale white hand which moved towards him, touched his hair and on so doing immediately vanished. **W.A.**

Darley Abbey

In 1137 some land on the north-east side of Derby was donated to a community of Augustinian canons on which they built a chapel dedicated to St Helen. Several years after this more land was granted to them near the banks of the River Derwent by the 2nd Earl of Derby, Robert de Ferrers, who took the new monastery under his wing, granting it further land and churches at Uttoxeter and Crich as well as the perpetual right to send a cart daily to collect timber from Duffield and Chaddesden.

The new abbey was to take many years to build and the people of Derby seemed to do all they could to help in its construction. First the area, which was covered in thick woodland, was cleared by the locals. Once this was completed, the order's own carpenters, masons, and craftsmen began the serious construction of the abbey.

The abbey was eventually completed some time around the mid-12th century and was dedicated to the Virgin Mary. Around the same time the canons moved to the new abbey from the Oratory of St Helen's in Derby. The outbuildings, kitchens, bakehouse, barns, workshops and even all the accommodation were almost certainly not finished until several years after the main abbey's completion.

Within 100 years Derby Abbey became a powerful establishment, playing host to the rich and poor. The greater part of the abbey's income came from the churches and lands affiliated to it. Rent was charged for land owned and leased by the abbey, fees for baptism, marriage and the tendering of the dead also brought in a significant amount of income. Gifts of land, perhaps in the hope of buying some redemption in the next life, continued to be given to the abbey and at the height of its wealth at the beginning of the 16th century, the abbey owned manor houses, churches and parcels of land in most parts of Derbyshire and several parts of Nottinghamshire.

The religious and political upheaval of the Reformation in the 16th

The Abbey public house, haunted by the ghost of a monk in a brown habit.

century, which gave birth to the Protestant Church, was brought about in England when King Henry VIII did away with the Pope's authority and proclaimed himself 'supreme head of the church'. This meant that most towns were to lose their monasteries. In 1536, Henry's Chancellor, Thomas Cromwell, sent representatives to take charge of the smaller priories and shortly after that the bigger ones followed. Derby Abbey was eventually dissolved and the monks given pensions, some of them reasonably generous, in accordance with their rank. The pensions were assessed by Sir John Port and William Cavendish, shortly after which the monastery was handed over and the official deeds signed in the presence of

Cromwell's representative. The religious orders disappeared from the streets of Derby and the monasteries taken down. Any valuables were commandeered and lands redistributed among Henry's favoured few.

Several ghosts are said to haunt the village of Darley Abbey, including two monks, a spectre that haunts a stretch of the River Derwent and a white lady seen near the Abbey public house. The following story was related to me by a former resident of Abbey Lane, Thomas Shellot, who informed me of the following:

"Shortly after moving into our new home in Abbey Lane, Darley Abbey, strange things began to happen. Work tools I had momentarily put to one side were gone when I went to pick them up seconds later. Strange banging noises and scratching sounds were frequently heard coming from the upper regions of the house.

"The main bedroom of the house was where the strangest occurrences took place. On retiring to bed I was often awoken from my sleep to find the figure of a monk, in what appeared to be a black habit, standing in the furthest corner of the room smiling at me. As soon as I fixed my concentration on him he would vanish and a cold breeze would seem to go through the room.

"Obviously it alarmed me greatly and by the fourth or fifth time that it happened I thought that I was going mad. Then one morning at breakfast, I noticed that my wife, who I had not told about my strange experience for fear of frightening her, looked very tired. I asked whether she was feeling unwell and she blushed and looked embarrassed. Further questioning revealed that for the previous three nights she had not slept very well. It was at this point that I decided to tell her about my experience and on hearing what I had to say the colour from her face visibly drained as she exclaimed, 'Oh my goodness, that's been the reason why I have been unable to sleep!'

"It transpired that my wife had also been disturbed from her sleep to find the same monk smiling down at her. The same thing happened on the second night and by the third night she was too upset and frightened to go to sleep for fear that the same thing might happen again. So tired was my wife by 2am that she eventually fell asleep regardless and was eventually awoken by someone calling her name. Sure enough, the monk was in the room and, as she watched him, he seemed to glide across the room, reach out, touch her, smile and then vanish into thin air.

"After the ghostly monk had appeared to my wife and touched her, he never reappeared. The strange banging noises and scratching sounds, however, continued and were still happening right up until we left the property."

These experiences were not unique to Mr and Mrs Shellot, for other households in the area have also felt and seen the presence of a ghostly monk. Several people have been disturbed from their sleep in the dark hours of the morning to find the monk in their room smiling at them. One lady, who we shall call Sue, informed me that a monk would often wander through her living room and walk through the wall.

Several of the houses in the area have what are believed to be remains of the abbey beneath the earth within their gardens. Sue, who has often seen the monk in her garden, believes that her house was built on the foundations of the former abbey as she has often heard distant music and what seems to be monks chanting.

Other ghosts have been seen at Darley Abbey including the 'River Ghost'. This spectre has been seen by several people at different times of the day and year. The ghost is said to be that of a man who always appears rowing a boat. He is seen in the centre of the river, sometimes rowing downstream, sometimes rowing against the current, often with a dog

Several phantoms have been seen on this stretch of the river at Darley, close to where the Derby Abbey once stood.

and always wearing a hat. I am informed that his style of dress is of an old and curious fashion.This particular river ghost is one of many that are said to be frequently seen on a stretch of river between Darley Abbey and the Holmes Recreation Ground, near Northcliffe House, home of the *Derby Evening Telegraph*.

One very interesting story comes from a lady called Janet who had a strange experience in the summer of 1984, whilst out for a walk with her boyfriend one warm sunny evening. Janet, who describes herself as 'down to earth', had decided that it would be a nice idea to go for a walk, as the weather had been particularly sunny and warm that day. Both Janet and her boyfriend Tim, decided that it would be a good idea to follow the River Derwent for a mile or so. This they did, starting from the River Gardens until they reached the Silk Mill, at which point Janet glanced towards the river and noticed the following:

"It was as if my eyes clouded over with a milky haze and there in the centre of my focus were two boys splashing about in the water. At first I

thought that they were two young lads having a swim, but as I watched I realised, to my horror, that this was not the case. From what I could see they were fully clothed in a style which seemed old and scruffy. They appeared to be about seven or eight years of age and one had mousey coloured hair and the other boy seemed darker of hair and complexion.

"Suddenly I became aware of them screaming for help and it was all that I could do to restrain myself from jumping into the water. The vision, which is the only word I can find to describe what I experienced, seemed to last for ages, although in reality it must have been, at most, 30 seconds. Although it was a lovely, bright, and warm evening, I felt an icy coldness creep over me. The experience made me feel quite sick and even though it happened over ten years ago, I can still remember it with clarity. I don't know who the boys were, I do realise, however, that they must have been ghosts. These young lads, I feel, have a connection with the Silk Mill and perhaps used to work there.

"I've visited the Silk Mill several times over the ensuing years and although I feel extremely uneasy, because I remember what I saw, I've never seen anything since. Sometimes I wish that I could see it again as there are occasions when I have questioned myself as to whether it really happened, then I remember my vision with clarity and know for sure that what I experienced happened for certain."

The other ghosts to haunt the River Derwent include strange unearthly

Derby River Gardens. Many ghosts haunt near here and strange lights have been seen hovering over the water.

and a sad looking man seen in the river near Holmes Recreation Ground and thought to be the ghost of a suicide victim.   **W.A.**

St Werburgh's Churchyard

The origins of the modern city of Derby probably lay beneath St Werburgh's Church in Cheapside. The Saxons sailed down the River Derwent and established a little village called Northworthy and dedicated a wooden church to their saint, Werburgha. There has been a church on that site ever since.

A dark stain appears on one page of

screams heard near St Mary's Bridge, a Roman soldier, a ghost that runs on the water, strange and curious lights seen hovering over the River Gardens

St Werburgh's Church as it must have looked in 1817 when the ringleaders of the Pentrich Revolution, the last three people to be hanged, drawn and quartered in England, were buried in an unmarked grave in St Werburgh's Churchyard.

St Werburgh's history. In 1322, Hugh Meynell of Langley violently shed blood in the church, not only committing injury to his victim, but sacrilege as well. This vile act put both the church and community against him. No building so defiled could be used for religious services until elaborate ceremonies of purification had been performed. These included public penance on the part of the culprit and the payment of large fines. Ever since that day, St Werburgh's appears to have been cursed and its stone tower fell down on 5 November 1601.

The head of the traitor Jeremiah Brandreth, who is buried in an unmarked grave in St Werburgh's Churchyard.

The body of the church collapsed twice more – in 1698 and then again in 1894, when the church building we know today was erected, although the tower is that of the 1601 building. Closed to worship in the early 1980s, St Werburgh's later became a shopping centre, but most of the business ventures within its walls eventually failed. Even the Dutch property developer who owned the church went bankrupt and at the time of writing the building is in the hands of the Official Receiver.

When St Werburgh's was being converted into shops, two of the workmen fell through the floor and landed in the crypt. In there were old, decaying coffins, some without lids. Many skeletons could be seen in those coffins. The workmen were so shocked, it took them five days to come back to work.

In 1817, the ring-leaders of the Pentrich Revolution, the last three people to be hanged, drawn and quartered in England, were buried in an unmarked grave in St Werburgh's Churchyard. Soon after they were buried, a Derby baker called Pegg would put a sheet over his head and jump out from the back of the churchyard, frightening the Derby citizens. He became such a nuisance that he was eventually locked away in Derby Gaol.

Another historic link with St Werburgh's is that Samuel Johnson, the man who compiled the first dictionary, was married there although he had no obvious links with Derby. **R.F.**

The Nun's Bridge Apparition

After World War Two, Elsie Goodhead was walking home in the snow. She was a West Ender and had caught the last bus, which dropped her at Nun's Bridge at 9.30pm on a Tuesday. As she was walking over the bridge, she saw someone who looked like a nun in a habit walking in front of her. Mrs Goodhead saw that the nun's habit was billowing out in the wind. She wondered what nuns wore under their robes to keep them warm in such icy weather. She also noticed, as she got close to the nun, that she wore men's boots and that the laces were undone and trailing in the snow.

Elsie hurried to try to catch up with the nun so that she could see her face, but she failed to do this, as the nun walked faster than she did. The nun seemed about 6ft in height and eventually just disappeared in front of her eyes. Elsie was not frightened, in fact she walked back along the bridge, to see if there was any footprints in the snow, but to her astonishment there were only her own.   **R.F.**

St Mary's Bridge

"The verdict is that you and each of you be carried to the place whence you came and from there be dragged on a hurdle to a place of execution and be severely hanged but be cut down while you are still alive, that your privy members be cut off, that your bowels be taken out and burnt before your faces, that your bodies be divided into four quarters and that these be at the disposal of Queen Elizabeth I, and the Lord have mercy on your souls."

Three Roman Catholic priests, Robert Ludlam, Nicholas Garlick and Richard Sympson – the Derby Martyrs – were imprisoned within the chapel on St Mary's Bridge awaiting their barbaric execution. On 24 July 1588, it was carried out and the grisly remains were hoisted on to the roof of the chapel. This execution was the result of the relentless religious persecution by the Lord Lieutenant of Derbyshire, the Earl of Shrewsbury,

St Mary's Bridge where the tormented cries of the Derby Martyrs can be heard.

St Mary's Bridge pictured as it might have looked around 1820. A ghostly monk has been seen inside the chapel on the bridge.

during a time when life could be endangered by following the Catholic faith.

The only way over the River Derwent in Saxon times was by a stepping-stone bridge which was near the site of the present St Mary's Bridge; It was here, in 917AD that Princess Aethleflaeda led a Saxon army from Nottingham over the Derwent. Fighting spread into the streets of the town before the Viking foes were driven back, and a great Saxon victory was won.

Later a wooden pack-saddle bridge was erected, possibly on the orders of Aethleflaeda, in thanksgiving for her victory. In the 13th century, there was talk of the great bridge at Derby, the wooden bridge being replaced by one of stone. By 1326, a small chapel dedicated to St Mary had been built on the bridge and a chaplain was appointed to conduct sermons. A hermit lived in the chapel and relied on the alms of passing travellers and also the collection of the tolls.

In those days the road from Derby to Nottingham led down St Michael's Lane and across St Mary's Bridge. Once over the bridge the traveller was then into wild country as the surrounding area was still wooded and infested with both wolves and outlaws.

No wonder the townsfolk turned into the little chapel on the bridge for a silent prayer before crossing the river to plunge into the unfriendly countryside.

St Mary's Bridge is believed to be haunted by the ghost of a nun who has been seen crossing the river and also by a ghostly coach bearing Mary, Queen of Scots which is seen passing across the bridge and on into the town for what was her only night's stay in Derby. And on the anniversary of the execution of the tragic Derby Martyrs, ghostly cries of anguish and torment can still be heard echoing over the quiet dark waters of the River Derwent.   **R.F.**

St Peter's Churchyard

During Victorian times and earlier there stood in St Peter's Street, before the road was widened, three poplar trees. According to local legend there were once three brothers who lived close to St Peter's Churchyard in a small cottage. The three were brutally murdered and then buried in the churchyard.

Their killers were never brought to justice. It was said that when the wind blew in a particular direction the trees would be seen to wave from side to side, and the faces of the three murdered brothers would appear, one in the bark of each tree trunk. It was further believed by many that if you listened carefully you could hear the trees whispering the names of their killers in the wind. Another version of the story says that they whispered three words, one each, Justice! Justice! Justice!   **W.A. & R.F.**

St Peter's Churchyard (to the right), where three murdered brothers are said to be buried.

St Mary's Church, where the ghost of a priest has been seen.

St Mary's Church, Bridge Gate

St Mary's Church was built by Augustus Pugin, who also drew designs for the Houses of Parliament.

Before 1840, Catholics in Derby were allowed to worship only in the Catholic Chapel in Chapel Street, but with the large influx of Irish immigrants to Derby with the building of the railways, land was purchased on Bridge Gate for a new Catholic church. It was, incidentally, Pugin's the first Catholic church and although he designed over 100 churches altogether, St Mary's has always been considered his masterpiece.

The ghost of a priest has been seen on the right-hand side of St Mary's Church. The story goes that a newly-installed priest was coming down the stairs with three other priests. Arriving in the main church the new priest mentioned to the others that he had not realised that there would be four other priests there that day. The others looked confused and told him that he must be mistaken as they were only three and he now made four. The new priest looked shocked and told the others that they had not long been seated upstairs for their meeting when an older priest with grey hair had joined them. **R.F.**

Commercial Ghosts

Bennett's, Iron Gate

This is possibly Derby's oldest retailing premises, dating back to 1734, when the business was Weatherhead's. Bennett's has two entrances, the main one in Iron Gate and a smaller entrance in Full Street. There also used to be a warehouse and staff entrance in Full Street.

One morning a female member of staff opened up the premises in preparation for that day's business. She let herself into the rear entrance

Iron Gate in Derby, the scene of several haunted premises including the George Inn, Bennett's shop and a gift shop and restaurant. The thorough fare is pictured here in the latter half of the 19th century.

Iron Gate, looking south in 1858.

in Full Street and went to the machine to clock in. Sitting by the wall on a box was an old man. She looked at him and thought nothing of it and continued to clock in. She then went into the main shop to switch all the lights on, then she realised "I was the first one in!" So who was he? She turned around and went back to the place where she had seen him, but of course the old man was nowhere to be seen. **R.F.**

Haunted Eagle Centre

There is much dispute amongst historians as to whether a castle existed in Derby. Many people firmly believe that Derby did indeed have a castle at one time, and there is some documentary evidence suggesting that this was so.

According to legend a bloody battle took place on the site of the present Eagle Centre in Derby. Ethelfleda, the 'Lady of Mercia', wife of Ethelred, Earl of Mercia, took Derby by storm in August 917AD. The town at that time was held by the Danes and the battle seems to have been a very fierce affair resulting in many warriors being slain on both sides. During the assault, four of Ethelfleda's thanes were slain 'within the gates of the city' to suggests that the town was fortified.

One writer suggested the following:

The heroic figure of Ethelfleda, fighting the Danes.

Eagle Street before it was demolished to make way for the Eagle Centre. Did a grand castle once stand near here, and do ghosts of a battle to regain Derby from the Danes still haunt the area?

'That Derby possesses a castle in pre-Norman times is beyond dispute. There is reason to think that this great fortress-raising lady [*Ethelfleda*] constructed it . . . there are indications of its mounds in the space between the present East, Albion and Eagle Streets, and its site was probably on Cockpit Hill, which was formerly called Castle Hill. It had probably ceased to be a stronghold before the Norman Conquest. Hutton says the last remains of the castle at Derby vanished some 200 years before his time (1791). He thought it dated back to "the Roman government, when it became requisite to guard so considerable town with a castle, which had no other fortifications".

'Hutton continued: "It was possible that it fell by violence, and no time so likely as in the Wars of the Roses . . .The lords of Derby being of the House of Lancaster, when that house fell, the wrath of the House of York might discharge its vengeance on this castle". Vestiges of the old fortress were to be found, claims Hutton, "in Mrs. Chamber's orchard, on the summit of the hill. One of the mounds, 80 yards long, runs parallel with the house upon Cockpit Hill, perhaps 100 yards behind them also, parallel with those in St Peter's Parish, but twice the distance. This place of security then stood out of the town in an open field; no houses were near. It was guarded by the Derwent on one side, and on the other ran the London Road. This, I apprehend, was the chief approach, because the passage afterwards bore the name Castle Street. From thence also, the field towards the east, now Mr Borrow's Park, acquired the name of Castle Fields." '

No doubt the debate will continue as to where exactly, if ever, Derby Caste stood. Whilst many people are of the opinion that it rose above what is now Cockpit Hill, there are just as many people who believe it was possibly located in several other likely places.

Whether there was a castle or not, what is certain is that over the centuries the face of Derby was to change considerably. Domestic housing developments were to spring up all over the face of Derby, as Industrial Revolution unfolded in England. Several such developments were a group of streets – namely Bloom Street, Eagle Street, Devonshire Street, Albion Place and Albion Street – which were built near the alleged site of Derby Castle. Eventually these streets and the houses in them were considered unfit for continued human habitation and they were demolished to make way for a new covered shopping development as Derby tried to keep pace with similar developments in neighbouring towns and cities.

Today we know this site as the Eagle Centre, but although thousands of people use the shopping centre each week, it seems that very few are fully aware of what stood on the site previously. Even fewer people know that in the late 1970s and the early 1980s, strange poltergeist phenomena and ghostly sightings were rife in the Eagle Centre. This information was partly repressed for fear of an adverse effect on sales within certain chain stores.

It would appear to the writer that these ghostly occurrences were due to the fact that, not only was the Eagle Centre built on a site where previously a whole community of people had once existed, it was also built on what may have once been a bloody battlefield where many warriors may have lost their lives. Modern investigations into the paranormal hold fast to the belief that places often record, or in some way reserve energies, which at a later date plays itself back. Other researchers maintain that many souls of the living, having met with tragic and often untimely deaths, remain earthbound unable to pass over to the next world. Perhaps one of these theories pertains to Derby's Eagle Centre?

The following are accounts of some of the happenings that took place, witnessed by ordinary everyday Derby people with no reason to fabricate information concerning the haunting of the Eagle Centre. Most of the names of the witnesses and the shops concerned have been changed to protect certain individuals, other names have been kept the same – but all of the incidents are accurate as witnessed. The following concern six shops within the Eagle Centre.

Shop One

Sightings have been made since the shop opened in 1975, although none of the original staff remain: 'Sightings two weeks ago, perhaps typical. At 5pm, Mrs Sharp, the manageress, was at cash desk, (halfway down shop, opposite stairs). She looked up to see a shadowy figure go down the stairs. Apparently another assistant nearby saw this, but a subsequent investigation disclosed no one downstairs, staff or customer.' The figure was described as 'a black or colourless shadow but not on the wall, hunched figure with no face discernible – scarf or shawl around head, elderly, female, movement very smooth'.

Some time prior to this, a member of staff, ascending to the staff room, felt a presence behind her (it felt 'itchy and cold'), turned around to see a shadowy figure of an old lady behind her, which faded.

'Sightings and noises tend to be heard early morning or late in the day every two or three months.'

Two assistants, Ann and Jeanette, went into basement of clothes shop to sort out the clothes hangers. Mrs K, at the rear of the shop, heard laughing and giggling and thought they were at the front of the basement. Then everything went quiet and the ladies appeared at the top of the stairs, distressed and crying. They had heard a scream or howl, a few feet behind them from an open doorway. Noise was said to be 'higher rather than loud'. Their ears 'popped and tingled'.

On a Saturday morning two members of staff were in the basement of the shop when both experienced an icy cold feeling and became aware of a presence behind them. Turning around they expected to see another member of staff but no one was present. They immediately heard a scream, on one note which gradually died away and was, 'not unlike a woman screaming as if in pain'.

Shop Two

Early on this day, one lady had heard a rustling noise coming from the area of the stairs. Footsteps were heard, although this was not unusual as footsteps were heard nearly everyday.

The manager of the shop saw a long-haired girl leaning over merchandise racks at rear of store. On going to speak to her he found no one there and a thorough search revealed no one in that area.

Workers in the staff room reported hearing and seeing coat hangers swinging on racks. A new girl, unaware of strange phenomena reported seeing coat hangers swinging violently on a wall peg.

Staff heard the sound of crockery rattling and on investigating they found that cups and saucers had been laid out on a table 3ft away from where they are normally kept in a cupboard. An electric kettle, normally unplugged, was plugged in and the water near boiling point – all without action by staff. Later on that day the electric cooker was found to be switched on with all four rings red hot.

There are also accounts of previous workers at Shop Two: 'Objects commonly found missing, despite extensive searching – objects would reappear next morning on top of desk. Often experienced cold areas. Often sensed an atmosphere of unease. Frequently felt as if she was being watched. On several occasions Mary felt her bottom being pinched, and from the corner of her eye was aware of a shadowy form.

'She once hear a peculiar noise, as if someone was running a stick along the ironwork of the stairs. She often smelt the stale smell of cigar smoke upstairs.

'Another assistant, no longer working there, named Jill, came running downstairs one day. She had been vacuuming near the staff room when she saw, to the side of her, a man going into the staff room. She described him as having pin-striped trousers and black shiny shoes. Staff have often heard footsteps during the day when there has been no one there.

'Staff at the shop believe that it is haunted by a dentist who used to work at the back of the premises.'

Shop Three

In this shop there were two guitars stacked in two cupboard boxes, one above the other, near the counter at the rear of the shop. The top box fell or was pushed by unseen hands and hit the deputy manageress, Mrs Gina, on the head. One lady present at the time described it as 'flying across', saying that it could not have fallen naturally in that direction.

Over several months more strange happenings occurred. One day Mrs Gina was going upstairs when she noticed a shadow on the staff room floor as she passed. Thinking a colleague was in the room, she called

out and when there was no reply she investigated the room only to find no one in there.

On several occasions staff heard their names being called out, only to find no one had called them. The voice was said to be deep, a man's voice. The figure of a man in a dark suit was often seen going up the stairs.

Shop Four

Shortly after this shoe shop opened, it became apparent that strange events were occurring for which there was no logical explanation.

At first, because of the strange sounds and banging noises, staff thought that someone might have been trying to break in and they called the police who checked the premises on several occasions but could find no trace of anyone trying to break in and no explanation as to the peculiar noises.

One morning the manager arrived for work to find a basket of shoes had been emptied on to the floor. He called a window cleaner over and together they searched the building but found nothing else untoward. Every shoe was out of the basket, leaving it completely empty. The contents were all around the basket, the right way up, standing on their soles.

On another occasion the manager went downstairs and saw a young lady with long hair. He called to her several times, thinking she was his supervisor but received no answer. On returning to upper floor he discovered that no one had been down there. Before long so many people had seen this girl that they began to build a description of her. The ghost of the girl was said to be about 16 to 18 years of age with long hair and a pleasant but plain face. One night when the manager went to check the back door he heard laughter in the corner close to him, although no one was visibly present.

Eventually electrical appliances started switching themselves on, taps were found running and a strange coldness pervaded parts of the buildings in several shops.'

Clearly things were getting worse and in a determined bid to stop these hauntings, an expert in the field of ghosts was called in. It transpired that several other shops were having similar experiences and they had called in a security firm to invest-igate. Whilst the security people were present with staff members, they all simultaneously experienced the manifestation of the ghost of an old lady. Two of the shop staff were greatly upset by this.

The old lady appeared on several occasions and whilst alterations to the shop were taking place, a strange moaning noise was heard and con-tinued to be heard for several months afterwards.

After the alterations, staff in an adjacent shop reported seeing strange shadowy figures and hearing the sound of moaning. This led some staff to believe that the ghost of the old lady had moved, a belief reinforced by the fact that during alterations some of the walls and partitions were moved.

The final straw came when a cleaner heard a woman's voice screaming or wailing, almost like a dog in pain. It lasted for some seconds. She ran to the stairs and collapsed at the top, severely shocked. She subsequently gave in her notice – after many years' service – and was too scared to re-enter shop ever again. Two other girls were also present and experienced hearing the same noise. Most of the staff, including the cleaner, had seen things in the past which had not bothered them.

As staff were attending the distressed cleaner, another scream was heard. One assistant immediately picked up her keys, ran downstairs, and opened the fire door but on looking outside there was no one to be seen. Later this same lady explained that when she had gone to check the fire door in the basement she had noticed an extreme coldness.

Another very peculiar incident, this time happening to a former security guard, concerns a young child which was observed wandering around a closed shop. Whilst doing his routine security rounds, John was shocked to find, when glancing through a window of a well-known clothes shop, a small girl child of approximately four years old, dressed in what seemed to be a 'very old fashioned style', wandering the shop floor clutching what he believes to have been some sort of soft toy. John became startled by what he had seen, believing that somehow the child had become lost and had accidentally been locked in the shop. He immediately summoned other secur-ity guards, who brought the master key for the shop, they entered the shop and a thorough search was completed to reveal no one but themselves in the premises.

A great deal of joking took place after this event with John being criticised for being over-tired or imagining the whole episode, John, however, assures me that he is in no doubt that he saw the ghost of a young girl and will remember the incident with clarity for the rest of his life.

It was around this time that it was decided by higher management within the centre that professional help was definitely needed, and a specialist, familiar in dealing with poltergeists and ghostly phenomena, was called in to help. All staff were advised to keep a record of events and to report any strange incidents to a City Council official, who had taken charge of the situation. Copies of a pamphlets entitled *Your Poltergeists And How To Deal With It* were distributed amongst shop workers. The following is an excerpt:

A: Its History.

1. Poltergeists are quite common and have been recorded for many hundreds of years.
2. At present cases are being researched and documented in the United States where the work of Dr Rhine of Duke University, and of Roll and the Morrises in England is noteworthy.
3. Many people down the ages and many today have and are suffering from the pranks of their poltergeist.

B: Its Nature

5. It is not an illusion and can produce physical effects which can be weighed, measured and recorded: i.e. it can move things and it can produce noises...
6. It is attached to and part of the mind of an owner or group of owners...
9. The poltergeist feeds on fear, although in fact it is harmless both to soul and body and is, in its way, a relief to the suffering mind.
11. Its 'owner' has no control over it and is unaware of his ownership.

C: How To Deal With It.

12. Once the pressures which have produced it are understood, the poltergeist will fade out.
15. Where premises have been effected, a ritual blessing will greatly help to calm the atmosphere of strain and fear.

Many members of staff from several of the shops experiencing problems did make themselves familiar with the pamphlet but the phenomena still continued and it was eventually decided that perhaps the only way to finally solve the ghostly dilemma was to hold a exorcism in the basement of one or more of the shops.

A meeting was arranged and the Bishop of Derby, along with several other clerical experts from Sheffield, was consulted on the matter and a meeting held in the basement of one of the haunted shops.

The result of the meeting was a decision that they would return and exorcise the building at the close of business one evening.

This allegedly took place in early December 1983. I am also informed that a further exorcism took place several months after the first one and

The Derby Playhouse, located within the Eagle Centre, has a ghost which manifests itself every so often.

was said to have worked better than the first.

The phenomena, however, was to continue for some time afterwards, although initially the ghostly appearances in the Eagle Centre dwindled for many months. Even today many staff who work at the centre are convinced that they have seen a ghost and some even several spirits. The Derby Playhouse, located within the Eagle Centre, has a ghost which manifests itself every so often, around the toilets located within the main building. **W.A.**

The Main Centre

Yet another haunted place, located near the Eagle Centre, is the Main Centre which was known to be haunted by strange spirits. Several reports in local newspapers in 1982 revealed how a health centre was being plagued by malevolent spirits awakened by two young girls who had decided to hold a seance in the building. During the seance the glass used was said to have 'gone wild', moving around and around the board frantically even though the two girls had taken their hands of the recepticle.

Shortly after the seance, strange things began to happen in the building, curious cold spots and thick atmospheres were sensed. One lady experienced being pushed along by an invisible force, which upset her a great deal. Another worker at the building told how she had seen a strange dark figure hiding in the storeroom. When she looked further, however, it had vanished with no possible means of getting past her as the room was small and the door visible to her all the time.

A night-time vigil was held by the health club manager, several newspaper reporters, and a lady who claimed to be a medium. A second seance was held, this time with the use of a Ouija board but with little or no effect. Workmen converting the building also experienced strange sightings and curious sounds. At present the ghosts within this building are said to be quiet, and the present owners and employees are quite happy for them to remain that way. **W.A.**

Number 22 Iron Gate

Now a restaurant, gift shop and sweet shop, in former days this was the town house of the Meynells – the famous family who introduced the Meynell Hunt into Derbyshire. Upstairs on the first floor, the ghostly apparition of a nun in a grey habit

No 22 Iron Gate. A ghostly nun watches people while they eat.

has been seen in the restaurant on frequent occasions, standing in the corner of the room, watching those within enjoying their meal.

Downstairs in the gift shop, a ghostly presence is often felt, the temperature dropping dramatically as staff go from one room to another. They sense that someone is standing with them, though no one can be seen or felt. Many of the staff have felt the hair on the back of their necks rise as they sense that they are not alone in the shop.   **R.F.**

Derby Grammar School

Now the Derby Heritage Centre in St Peter's Churchyard, this was originally built around 1580 to accommodate a new school opened under a charter from Mary Tudor. It educated Derby's boys for nearly 300 years, including Joseph Wright, the world-famous Derby painter, the Revd John Flamsteed, the first Astronomer Royal, and the Revd John Cotton, Pilgrim Father and founder of Boston, Massachusetts. Some say that the building was erected on part of St Peter's Church burial ground, although it seems rather strange, given all the land available at the time, that the authorities would choose to build the school on top of a graveyard. Admittedly, though, three bodies have been found beneath the floor of the building and since they were disturbed, strange happenings have occurred: a poltergeist has been reported, which piled furniture upon tables; footsteps are often heard upstairs in what would have been the old dormitory; doors bang, and when security cameras were being installed at 3.30am, one of the workmen saw a young boy of about ten years old with long fair hair standing in front of him. The workman refused to work upstairs unless his colleague accompanied him wherever he went.

R.F.

Taylor, Simpson & Mosley, Solicitors, St Mary's Gate

These premises are one of the finest town houses in the city of Derby. The building is haunted by a lady dressed in a blue Georgian costume. Mrs Shipley, who many years ago was an office junior, was distributing a tray of tea one morning to the various solicitors' offices. She was going up the staircase on the extreme right of the building when she saw a lady in blue standing at the top of the stairs waiting to come down.

Mrs Shipley hurried up the stairs to a recess where they could both pass and the mysterious lady started to walk down the staircase. The phantom stopped by a window and it was only then that Mrs Shipley realised that she could still see the window even though the lady was

The haunted staircase at 35 St Mary's Gate. The ghost of a woman has been seen several times, standing by the window.

standing in front of it. She dropped the tray of tea she was carrying and ran back to the basement where her colleagues her asked if 'she had seen a ghost' as she looked so pale.

"I have" she replied, "on the top of the stairs." They told her not to worry as this ghostly lady had frequently been seen in the past and had never hurt anyone.

Mrs Shipley still visits the building and is happy to show people the window where she once saw the ghost of a Georgian lady.

R.F.

Interior of 35 St Mary's Gate pictured in the 19th century, today the premises of Taylor, Simpson & Mosley, solicitors.

Lock-Up Yard

The area now occupied by Derby's Fish Market, in Lock-Up Yard, was originally the old police lock-up. In 1879, a policeman was murdered there. Gerald Mannering was the son of a Staffordshire gentleman, but was a ne're-do-well, whose father was about to 'send him to the colonies'.

The Lock-Up Yard pictured in the 1930s. When the area to the left of the Market Hall door was demolished in the 1950s, some of the cells, complete with their stone sinks and hard benches, were exposed to shoppers' view.

Mannering came to Derby and bought a revolver and 50 rounds of ammunition before taking himself on a drinking spree around the town and stealing a pony and trap. He was arrested in the yard of the Traveller's Rest public house at the top of Ashbourne Road and charged with the driving of a pony and trap while drunk. He was brought back to the police lock-up, but no one searched him and he was able to produce his revolver, wounding an inspector and shooting dead PC Moss.

Eventually, Mannering was sentenced to be hanged for the murder of the policeman but in those days the fledgling *Derby Daily Telegraph* shared Lock-Up Yard with the police station and an employee of the newspaper heard the policemen claiming that Mannering had been found guilty on the toss of a coin. He told the editor of the paper, who reported the staggering allegation to the Home Secretary. A subsequent enquiry established that the jury was split 50-50 over Mannering's guilt and hat they had, indeed, drawn lots to see who would be the foreman and thus have the casting vote. The sentence of hanging was commuted to one of life imprisonment. To this day they say that PC Moss still haunts the area of the old police lock-up and has been seen by various fishmongers there and also by John Boulton, who was a florist in the Market Hall.   **R.F.**

46 Queen Street

This was for many years the premises of John Nelson Hefford & Sons, boot makers and footwear retailers. It was customary in those days for many shop owners to live on or behind the premises and Carl Hefford and his wife lived behind their shoe business (*see photograph on page 66*). One night in 1920, just before they were going to bed, they heard a tremendous commotion going on in the shop. They could hear the sound of shoe boxes and shoes being thrown around the shop, and the rustling of tissue paper in which the shoes were wrapped.

Mr Hefford was convinced that there were burglars within the shop and told his wife to go out of the back door and fetch the police.

She returned with an officer and the policeman stood in front of the shop window and heard the commotion that was going on inside. He shouted to Carl to open the back door and switch on the lights. This he did, whilst the policeman broke into the shop from the front. All was calm and peaceful inside. Not a shoe box was out of place, not a shoe was out of its box. None of those present could not believe what they had heard.

Years later, when Queen Street was widened, the old shoe shop of Carl Hefford was demolished and underneath the premises were found what were believed to be the remains of Derby's 'lost' church, St Mary's. This is where St Mary's Gate gets its name. Nine graves were found with skeletons still in their coffins under what was though to be the nave of the church – directly underneath Carl Hefford's shop.   **R.F.**

Smith's Factory

A ghostly night-watchman is believed to haunt the former Smith's clothing factory at Drewry Lane, near Abbey Street, Derby. A former worker at the factory informed me that he and colleagues had regularly seen the ghost from a bedroom window which overlooked the back of the factory. After the closure of Smith's the building was converted into luxury studio-style apartments. Several tenants have informed me that on many occasions they have heard and seen strange things. One tenant is adamant that on numerous occasions, whilst climbing the stairs to her apartment, she has been pinched, on one occasion on the bottom, by unseen hands.

Another former worker at the factory, who was a watchman, told me that on several occasions he had seen the ghost and was quite used to seeing him. In the end the watchman would just simply say 'Goodnight' and continue with his nightly security checks on the factory. Even though this ghost seems to have been active in more recent times, there are few people who have seen him of late.

Another house on Drewry Lane, a one-time farmhouse, is reputed to be haunted by the ghost of a white lady who has been seen on several occasions, by the owner, moving around a particular room in the house "As if on roller skates". **W.A.**

The County Hotel

To the left of the Shire Hall was an inn known as the County Hotel or King's Arms. Indeed, the coat-of-arms can still be seen above the building. It was simply an inn sign although many local people think that it was connected with the court building which stood next door. Jurors, barristers and the friends and

The former King's Head County Hotel. In the 18th century, a serving girl was murdered in this hotel and her ghost has been seen by many people in the building

relatives of the people attending the courts were put up in this building. More recently the building was used by the Derbyshire Constabulary.

In the 18th century, a serving girl was murdered in this hotel and her ghost has been seen by many people in the building. **R.F.**

The Derby Hippodrome

In 1913, Derby Hippodrome was opened in Green Lane. It offered music-hall style entertainment, variety shows and that sort of thing, and many famous names appeared there including Flanagan and Allen. Legend has it that whilst sheltering 'underneath the arches' of the Great Northern Railway in Ford Street, they were inspired to write their famous song. Their version – obviously to be accepted – was that although they wrote the song in Derby, they had been inspired by some railway arches in London.

On the site of the Hippodrome there originally stood a private mental asylum where one of the inmates cut a warder's throat, resulting in the asylum being closed shortly afterwards. The ghostly form of this unfortunate warder has been seen in the Hippodrome - today it is a bingo club – staggering and clutching his throat to stem the flow of dark sticky blood which he appears covered in.

Also present within the building is the ghost of a young girl who has been heard crying when the public has gone. It has been claimed that a little girl once lost her teddy bear

Derby Hippodrome, haunted by several ghosts. It stands on the site of an old lunatic asylum.

over the balcony, reached over to stop it from falling, stumbled and fell to her death in the stalls below and to this day her cries may still be heard echoing throughout the building. **R.F.**

Principles Clothing Store

This shop standing in St Peter's Street is haunted by a man wearing a long coat who is always seen without legs in the vicinity of the upper regions of the building. Perhaps the reason to him being 'legless' is the fact that the building has now changed and the floor is higher than it was at the time of this particular ghost's physical death. **R.F.**

Debenham's Department Store

This large store is said to be haunted by no less than 17 ghosts, including a grey lady, a poltergeist, a ghostly figure in a storeroom and crockery being hurled about. One girl, Marie Tillotson, was pushed quite hard down some stairs by an unseen hand. Although the present building is quite modern – it was redeveloped from the former Ranby's shop – it occupies the site of many old buildings which would once have teemed with life. It stands on the corner of Green Lane and Victoria Street. Until 1838, Victoria Street was called Brookside and Markeaton

The junction of Green Lane and Victoria Street pictured in early Victorian days. This is now the site of Debenham's store, said to be haunted by no less than 17 ghosts.

Brook still flows underneath the Strand, Victoria Street, beneath the old medieval bridge of St Peter's, under Albert Street and joins the River Derwent in the River Gardens.

W.A. & R.F.

Surgical Spirits

Derbyshire Royal Infirmary

Not suprisingly considering the nature of establishments – more often than not tending to the very sick and dying – the majority of hospitals within the city of Derby are said to be haunted by spirits not at rest – from grey ladies to phantom children and even the ghost of a screaming lady who committed suicide by hanging herself from one of the staircases in the main building of one hospital.

The Derbyshire Royal Infirmary is said to be haunted by several ghosts, the main two being a grey lady who wanders the hallways and wards checking patients, the other being a doctor who is said to have fallen to his death down a lift shaft near two of the wards on the western side of the building. The former ghost is affectionately referred to as 'Florrie', having been named so by several nurses who believe her to be a sort of Florence Nightingale figure if not the Lady with the Lamp herself. Strange cold spots and sudden gusts of icy wind have also been experienced by

Derbyshire Royal Infirmary in about 1896. Does the ghost of Florence Nightingale patrol the wards at night?

Statue of Florence Nightingale at Derbyshire Royal Infirmary, where one ghostly figure is affectionately known as 'Florrie'.

several nursing staff on the main corridor and several of the wards which adjoin it.   **W.A.**

The Gibbet Ghost

It is believed that the site of the Derbyshire Royal Infirmary once housed a gibbet used for exhibiting the bodies of executed criminals. One famous story describes how a criminal, who committed a heinous murder, had the last laugh on some of those people glad to see him hanged for his terrible crime.

On the last Monday before Christmas in 1774, a small party of workmen trudged along Full Street to begin a cold and dreary day's work. As the men passed one of the larger old houses they heard desperate screams and looked up to see a woman frantically waving from an attic window. The workmen quickly broke down the door and rushed to the top of the house where they were met by the hysterical woman who had waved from the window and who led them to one of the bedrooms on the upper floor.

What met their eyes was a terrible scene. On the bedroom floor lay the badly beaten body of the elderly resident of the house, a Mrs May Vickers, her fingers red and scratched, where the many rings which she normally wore had been torn from her hand. The young servant lady reiterated to the workmen that in the early hours of the morning she had been awoken by her mistress's shouting. On reaching the bedroom of Mrs Vickers she was met by the figure of a man dressed in dark clothes. The man had told the servant to go back to her room, threatening her with death if she dared come out again. There she had waited until dawn and she managed to attract the attention of the workmen.

Police inquiries revealed Mrs Vickers' murderer to be a man named Matthew Cocklane, a local worker to the area. Further investigations revealed that he had taken flight to Ashbourne, and then on to Leek where he had taken a post-chaise to Liverpool. Nothing more was heard of Cocklane until nearly a year later when he was tracked down and arrested in Dublin.

Matthew Cocklane was brought back to Derby amid much excitement and curiosity from the locals and taken straight before the local magistrates to face a murder charge, about which he denied all knowledge.

Mrs Vickers' maid was called to

Full Street earlier this century. It was here that Matthew Cocklane carried out the terrible murder of Mrs May Vickers.

identify her mistress's murderer and she said that she recognised his voice. On this evidence and that of several other testimonies, Matthew Cocklane was tried and found guilty at Derby Assizes in March 1776, and was sentenced to death by hanging.

Shortly before Cocklane was executed, he made a full confession stating that he had entered his victim's house by forcing his way through a window and on discovering Mrs Vickers he beat her to death with an iron pin. After forcing Mrs Vickers' rings from her fingers, Cocklane then stole a bag of gold worth £300 and made his way out of the house and then on to Ashbourne, through to Leek and eventually Ireland.

Cocklane's day of execution arrived and he was led to the gallows accompanied by a Methodist preacher who constantly prayed for the condemned man's soul. A large crowd had gathered, many of whom looked forward to such a gruesome event.

It was a custom that the body of the executed criminal be handed over to local surgeons for dissection. At the request of 'some gentlemen of the town', however, the body of Matthew Cocklane was instead tarred and hung in chains at the Bradshaw Hay, which is believed to be the present day junction of Bradshaw Way and London Road. This type of practice was common at the time as a warning to would be wrongdoers of their likely fate should they break the law.

A few nights after Cocklane's body was hung at Bradshaw Hay, a strange wager was struck amongst several young men at the Green Dragon in St Peter's Street, that one of the company dare not climb a ladder to the gibbet and offer Cocklane's putrefying body a bowl of warm broth.

As the clock struck midnight the young man who had accepted the bet climbed the ladder to the gibbet and holding aloft a steaming bowl of broth said: "Matthew, thy must be cold up there. Here's a basin of broth to warm thy bones!"

From the dark and cold night air, a voice boomed back at him, "Well blow on it then!"

The young man who had offered the corpse the bowl of broth fell from the ladder in horror and ran off along London Road much to the amusement of his colleagues.

Hidden at the foot of the gibbet was a well-known Derby ventriloquist named Squeaking Jemmy.   **W.A.**

Mickleover Manor, Etwall Road

Having had several uses in its time and once belonging to the Newton family before becoming a boys' school and then a psychiatric hospital, the estate of Mickleover Manor was eventually sold off and consisted of much land including 'many dairy farms and small-holdings'.

Having been extended and modernised in part, the building itself has much warmth and character. The present house is believed to have been built around the middle of the 19th century although I am informed that a much older house,

Mickleover Manor, where a mysterious lady is often seen wandering around the grounds.

by several ghosts. When it functioned as a hospital it was believed by many nurses to be haunted by a caped figure which was often seen in the upper regions of the house. Another ghost is said to be that of a nurse who, according to local legend, died in the building as the result of an accident around the time of World War Two. It is believed by some that part of the building was bombed or hit by shrapnel during the war, killing a nurse, although there is no substantive evidence.

Other ghosts inhabit the building, all, I am informed, of a friendly disposition. One particular phantom known as the 'Caped Lady' is seen descending the main staircase to walk through the main front door and proceed casually into what little remains within the grounds of a once-great medieval forest. Several minutes after she vanishes into the trees she reappears and re-enters the house.

Other people who have worked at the building during its long history informed me that they had sometimes witnessed strange 'mists' which would suddenly appear and then vanish again as quickly. Others maintained that the staircase was the most haunted spot, being quite often frequented by intense cold spots and, according to one lady, haunted by a disembodied pale hand of a lady which she had often seen clutching

Wooden carving on a staircase at Mickleover Manor. The disembodied hand of a woman has been seen clutching the staircase.

probably wooden, existed on the site previously and materials may have been brought from other areas.

The building is said to be haunted

The Manor Hospital, since demolished, on Uttoxeter Road. Some nurses reported seeing ghosts here.

one of the carved figures of a griffin on the staircase.

Other stories abound concerning the history and ghosts of the building, including a secret passage leading to the nearby church of All Saints', a strange tree within the grounds on which the distorted face of a devil may be seen, and strange lights seen hovering within the building. At the time of writing, the fate of this building, is uncertain.　　　**W.A.**

The Manor Hospital, Uttoxeter Road

Now demolished, to be replaced by yet another supermarket and a

The Manor Hospital, Uttoxeter Road, was once a workhouse (pictured here) and then hospital. It was reputed to be haunted by numerous ghosts including a poltergeist in the area at the back of the hospital near Ward 7, known as 'The Back Block'.

restaurant and 'motel' complex, the former workhouse and then hospital was reputed to be haunted by numerous ghosts including a poltergeist in the area at the back of the hospital near Ward 7, known as 'The Back Block'.

The hospital was said to be haunted by a former night sister, who was frequently seen wandering the corridors. One former night sister at the hospital, Josephine Riley, informed me that she had often seen the ghost of the night sister and had also once been witness to items being thrown around the dormitory of Ward 7 by a poltergeist.

After the closure of the hospital in 1988, stories began to surface from security watchmen concerning the strange smell of smoke often experienced within the building. One workman reported seeing the figure of a small lady in the vicinity of what would have been the kitchens. This same workman also heard singing coming from what was the chapel. The singing continued until the door to the room was opened, at which

point the singing stopped abruptly and on entering the chapel the watchman found the room to be quite empty apart from himself.   **W.A.**

Pastures Hospital

I have heard ghost stories concerning nearly every ward at the Pastures Hospital, ranging from the 'ordinary' to the extremely bizarre, from grey ladies to strange oval-eyed creatures seen lurking within the bushes in the grounds. Pastures Hospital, now closed, perhaps houses as many reputed ghosts as one would care to count.

Built in the middle of the 19th century, the land on which it is stood was said to have been gifted to the people of Derby by two brothers to serve as a sanatorium. Originally it boasted turrets but these were removed earlier this century; whilst still intact they would have made this building perhaps one of the most impressive in the area.

Perhaps the most sinister ghost to haunt the area around the building is a screaming grey lady who was seen and heard on several occasions by former workers at the hospital. The hospital was also the scene of

Pastures Hospital. One ward was the scene of such a terrifying spectre that several nurses asked to be moved.

several poltergeists which terrorised staff shortly before the hospital closed. One particular poltergeist was known to have thrown objects around a ward and to remove medical equipment and accessories, often returning them days or weeks later into locked storage rooms with limited access to staff.

One particular ward, known as Wessington, was the scene of a more terrifying spectre which upset nurses so much that several of them asked to be moved. So frightening were some of the incidents that eventually a vicar was called in and the ward was exorcised. This subdued the mischievous spirit but not for long as strange occurrences soon returned, only this time worse. Once a community of nurses and residents, the former county asylum now has a sad, forlorn air as it awaits commercial and residential development.

One other interesting story concerning Pastures Hospital comes from a lady who had worked there for many years as a nurse. Lolita Beachcroft, a local to the area, reiterated to me her account of a curious

incident which happened to her in a very old building, once used as a ward, and known then as Beech House:

"I had locked up areas of the building, as the ward routine, prior to the night staff arriving for duty. On reaching the upper regions of the building I went to a particular room which was then used by the consultant psychiatrist. He was in the habit of taking a drink of tea prior to ending his day's work and we, the nurses, would collect his empty cup so it would be washed and clean ready for his use the next morning.

"Having done a quick tidy-up and collected the relevant rubbish to be thrown away, I made my way out of what was essentially, compared with many of the rooms in the building, a very small room. Arriving at the door – the only door to the room – I put the lights off and closed the door.

"But as I placed my key into the lock, I was shocked to hear, from just behind the other side of the door of a now empty room, the sound of eerie laughter – loud and very clear. Needless to say I immediately went back downstairs to the other staff nurse and told them of my experience. The other nurses accompanied me back to the room but on unlocking the room and looking inside we found nothing untoward.

"Several days after this event the consultant approached me and asked me about my experience. Apparently one of the other nurses had mentioned to him what had happened. The consultant asked me if I was pregnant to which I replied no. Thinking this a strange question I asked him why he had asked me such an odd question. 'My dear', he replied, 'These experiences are quite common when ladies are pregnant. The sensitivity in many cases are heightened, often resulting in them experiencing unusual or psychic phenomena of an unexplainable kind'."

The consultant asked Lolita if she would be prepared to accompany him back to the room and wait patiently with a tape recorder to see if any unusual sounds or indeed the strange laughter could be recorded, Lolita declined, preferring not to hear the sinister laughter again.

Many other ghost stories abound from nurses who once worked at the Pastures Hospital. Out of the many stories that I have heard, the most common seems to concern dying patients and the ghosts of dead relatives apparently coming in the dying person's last minutes, almost as if to collect the departing soul and accompany it to whatever place it might go. It was customary with many nurses, indeed in most hospitals, to open a window after finding a patient dead. This custom was carried out, I am informed, so that the spirits of the dead do not stay in the building but take flight to the next life. The custom of placing fresh flowers near the recently departed and not touching the body for at least an hour out of respect was yet another ritual practised at many hospitals.

There are many other strange stories concerning ghosts and the paranormal, alas too numerous to mention here. One thing, however, is certain: Pastures Hospital as was, from all accounts, the most haunted hospital, if not the most haunted building in Derby, and indeed the Derbyshire area.

Another two annexes of what was the Pastures Hospital are also said to be haunted – Rykneld House and Shirley House, one still functioning clinically. The former is now a private boys' school and is believed to be haunted by a white lady who is seen wandering in what is known as 'The Gallery', on upper floors of the house. Many nurses who saw her say that she carried a lamp while others maintain that she exudes a phosphorous glow. The lake within the grounds of the building is also said to be haunted by the ghost of a previous heiress who drowned within its murky waters.

Shirley House is situated on South Street and is believed by some to be haunted by the ghost of a warder and his wife. These two ghosts are said to be connected with the adjacent former County Gaol in Vernon Street, now derelict, and it is also believed that a secret passage, one of many thought to be in the area, leads from this building to the old gaol.   **W.A.**

Haunted Inns

Seymour's Wine Bar

Tucked away in St Werburgh's Churchyard, behind the former church off Cheapside, is Seymour's Wine Bar and Restaurant which is known to be haunted by the figure of an old lady, dressed in grey, who is said to frequent the upper regions of the property. Several stories have been related to me concerning the appearance of this ghost and many of the sightings are said to be 'pre-announced' by the smell of lavender, which pervades the room to the extent of 'stinging the nostrils' as one young lady described it.

Seymour's Wine Bar. The ghost of an old lady often walks the upstairs areas of this building, accompanied by the smell of lavender.

Several strange incidents took place in the building when a former manager lived there. On several occasions he would find that cutlery had been moved around and placed in a different order. Other items would occasionally disappear, only to reappear at a later date, sometimes in the same place, often in a totally different location, days or weeks later.

The area known as the 'Bake House', in the upper regions of the building, was often reported by staff to have a 'watchful presence'. On several occasions staff felt themselves being touched by unseen hands, but never did anyone feel that they were meant any harm. In fact, all the employees were quite happy with their unseen guests.

The adjacent graveyard of St Werburgh's is also said to be haunted by several spirits and one former worker at Seymour's informed me that on several occasions he had seen the figure of a man appear to walk through the wall into the building. **W.A.**

The White Lion

A former 17th-century coaching inn which was known as the White Lion on the junction of Friar Gate and Ashbourne Road was the scene of an unfriendly and malevolent presence which made life difficult for the owner of the building – which had by then become a small restaurant – eventually attacking him and causing him great discomfort.

The property was said to be haunted by more than one presence and the most predominant were those of a man and woman. The man was thought to be angry, aggressive, dressed in a light shirt, dark trousers

The White Lion at the corner of Brick Street and Ashbourne Road, pictured before the turn of the century. A malevolent spirit made life unsettling for a later owner of the building.

and brown leather waistcoat. The woman was believed to be kind, considerate, of 18th-century appearance, wearing a black skirt, white blouse with a brooch and a 'cutaway' jacket. Her hair was said to be swept back from her forehead, giving her a most pleasing countenance.

Friends and visitors to the property also claim to have experienced the ghosts within the building. Several visitors stated that they could smell the scent of violets, whilst others claim to have seen shadowy figures at the rear of the premises.

The owner of the building told me some of his experiences whilst living at the property: "The other ghost was a much nastier character. On several occasions I was violently pushed against the doors of the building once used as a brewhouse. I never actually saw the ghost but the force behind the push it gave me was strong. When that particular ghost was around there was a definite 'thickness' in the air. My dog made terrible wailing sounds when in the vicinity of the brewhouse. Once she reeled backwards as though she had been kicked by some unseen presence. Thereafter she refused to go there after dark, even if I accompanied her".

One particular night the owner awoke to find the lady ghost standing over his dog which was sleeping on a chair in the bedroom, undisturbed and enjoying the ghostly visitor's presence. The lady was stroking the dog and when she realised that she was being watched she smiled at the owner and faded away. Never did he feel that she meant any harm, although the same could not be said for the male presence within the property.

It may be worth noting that violent incidents concerning ghosts and hauntings are extremely rare and unusual. Whilst many people will often state that they felt that there was an overbearing feeling of unease or malevolence, it is rare to encounter an individual who has been personally attacked and some schools of thought dealing with the paranormal would find this type of ghostly manifestations highly dubious.

W.A.

The Old Silk Mill public house. A ghost in Cavalier costume has been seen here.

The Wagon & Horses

Strange occurrences took place at the Wagon & Horses public house, Ashbourne Road, Derby. The ghost of a lady in blue was said to have been seen by the landlady in the upper regions of the pub. The landlady, a very down-to-earth person, not given to flights of the imagination, stated that she had seen the ghost whilst alone upstairs. The landlord, a self-confessed sceptic, admitted that he had not believed in such things until a picture, complete with a two-inch nail, had fallen, or been torn from the wall, by invisible hands whilst he was passing some uncomplimentary comments about whatever apparition the landlady may have seen upstairs.

W.A.

The Old Silk Mill

This pub is Full Street is known to be haunted by the figure of a Cavalier complete with feathered hat and sword, seen in the bar area of the pub. One gentleman, Michael, said that he had once seen the ghostly Cavalier, assuring me that he had been sober at the time. He recounted how he had walked into the pub early one evening in late summer to be passed by a man wearing a Cavalier-style clothing.

Believing that there might be a fancy-dress party that evening, he inquired at the bar and was informed that there was not. Michael then commented to the barmaid about the man in fancy dress, she looked back at him blankly, stating that she had not seen such a person. Michael concluded that he had, indeed, seen a ghost. Other people have also seen such a figure in or near the pub. Local legend states that a Cavalier had indeed been killed near this spot in a duel which is said to be re-enacted annually.

W.A.

109

The Vaults

A former landlady of this property in Iron Gate – formerly the Irongate Hotel, the Irongate Tavern, then Henry's, then Henley's and now P.J.Pepper's (what will it be next week?) – informed me that she had on several occasions experienced a feeling that she was not alone when in the cellars. Frequently she had felt that she was being watched and on one occasion saw someone dressed in dark colours vanish before her eyes. Customers to the pub have also seen and felt strange things in the lounge area, although, I was assured, for the greater majority of the time this public house has a more than welcoming atmosphere.   **W.A.**

The Lady In Grey

Although not within the city of Derby, the Lady In Grey restaurant at Shardlow is perhaps one of the most famous recorded haunted buildings local to the area. Many reference books on ghosts include the story of The Lady In Grey, making it the most widely-distributed local haunting.

This restaurant has been written about in several national books and nearly all of the stories I have read differ, some claiming that the building is haunted by several spirits and others claiming that only one ghost has been seen there.

Perhaps the most interesting story concerns the youngest of three sisters who was left a large amount jewellery by her mother. The elder of the sisters was jealous and in a fit of temper took the jewels and buried them in the gardens. The younger sister searched in vain and frequently implored her elder sister to tell her where they were hidden.

After several years the elder girl gave in and agreed to show her sister where she had buried the legacy. But so many new plants had grown and

The Lady in Grey restaurant at Shardlow is probably the most famous haunted building in the Derby area and is frequently mentioned in books published elsewhere. The most famous ghost here is that of a young heiress, searching for her inheritance.

blossomed in the garden that the elder sister found it impossible to remember where she had hidden them. To this day the ghost of the younger sister is seen looking for her lost inheritance and it is that ghost, which always appears in grey, which gave rise to the name of the restaurant.

When I visited the Lady In Grey restaurant in the spring of 1995, I was informed by the manager that the ghost of the young lady has not been reported for some time. She did, however, inform me that several other ghosts are said to haunt the building, and that on occasion the family's dogs had acted strangely. I was also told that previous owners of the building had experienced very strange happenings, including one gentleman owner who was locked into a walk-in freezer by unseen hands which pushed the doors shut. He was rescued by his wife who happened to be passing ten minutes later.   **W.A.**

The Dolphin

This is Derby's oldest public house, dating back to around 1530. Of course, due to its great antiquity, it has various ghosts associated with it including a blue lady who walks through the old lath and plaster walls. She has been seen by many customers in the pub and also in the tea rooms upstairs. The most intriguing part of the Dolphin is its 18th-century extension on the left-hand side of the building in Full Street. This was not always part of the Dolphin, being originally a doctor's house.

In the 18th century, it was customary for doctors to have bodies delivered to their homes for the furtherance of medical science. Part of the sentence of execution in those days was that afterwards, the body of the criminal would be delivered to 'ye surgeons' for dissection'. Many condemned prisoners were more in fear of the dissection then the death sentence.

Before the introduction of the new drop, around 1760, the victim was delivered to the hangman on a cart. The executioner then placed the halter around the victim's neck and the cart was driven away, leaving the condemned man swinging. It could take anything up to 20 minutes for the person to die of slow strangulation from the weight of their own body, unless, of course, the executioner happened to be feeling particularly generous, in which case he would climb to the top of the scaffold or tree and put both feet on the hanging person's shoulders and push down, or with his assistant, take a leg each – and this is where the saying 'pull the other leg' comes from – and pull down, thus tightening the rope around the neck and hastening the end.

Because of the length of time it sometimes took for the accused to die, some who were hanged and then delivered to the surgeons in the Shire Hall in St Mary's Gate, woke up on the dissecting slab.

These poor wretches would be taken off and placed in a corner where a careful eye was kept upon them to see if they would later die or recover. A particular incident of this kind apparently happened in the cellar under the doctor's house, which is now part of the Dolphin.

One morning, so we are led to believe, our doctor came eagerly down into the cellar after a body had been delivered. He pulled the body on to a table and ripped the shroud from it, only to find life still present. No one knows what happened – whether the doctor died from shock; whether the person died; or the doctor in fact plunged his scalpel into the body; or even if the person recovered – but many bodies were dissected in that cellar under the Dolphin, and to this day it is haunted by a poltergeist

The Dolphin, Derby's oldest pub, is associated with a number of ghosts. The 'corpse' of an executed man came back to life here as a surgeon prepared to dissect him in a cellar under the building.

which turns the taps of the beer kegs off in that part of the cellar.

Because of the unearthly atmosphere, two members of staff normally go down together, as no one wishes to venture there alone. **R.F.**

The Blessington Carriage

In 1976 this building, located in Chapel Street, was converted from two 19th-century cottages. It is believed to have been used at some time as a funeral parlour. There are also stories that at one time someone committed suicide by hanging themselves in one of the upstairs rooms. The ghostly figure of a depressed looking woman has been seen wandering the building on at

least two occasions. The pub's manager, Tony, was always extremely sceptical about the supernatural and ghosts, but so many of his employees have seen and experienced strange happenings that he is beginning to reconsider his initial feelings on the subject.

Heavy footsteps were heard at night in the upstairs function room. The cellar door was actually slammed shut and then some unseen force seemed to hold it closed, but when the staff finally did gain entry, the cellar was empty.

Glasses have mysteriously flung themselves off bar hooks and a bookcase smashed after flying across the bar and an old rug was slung across a doorway leading into the pub's rear storeroom although seconds before, the pub manager had passed through unimpeded.

The dog which lived there would often look down the bar as if he could 'see something', often with his hackles rising. He would run on to the dance floor and start barking at something no one else could see and then run back again. Sometimes the owner could not even get the dog to go on to the dance floor, even on a lead. Who or what was actually causing the hauntings has always been a mystery.   R.F.

The Bell Hotel

One of the old coaching inns in Derby, the Bell Hotel has managed to retain much of its original appear- ance, although its apparent Tudor timbering was not added until after World War One. It was built around 1680, for the Meynell family and is reputed to have various ghosts within. A Victorian lady in blue stands in one of the downstairs bars and vaporises in front of staff and customers alike. A poltergeist in another downstairs room has been known to throw items around, one barmaid being hit on the back of her head by a wooden coat- hanger, but close inspection of the room revealed no one else present.

Upstairs in the Bell, one of the rooms is haunted by the ghost of a serving girl who has been seen on frequent occasions, dressed in 18th- century clothing with a white mob cap. The original story, that she was murdered by the Jacobites in 1745,

The door to room 29 at the Bell Hotel, Sadler Gate, in which a serving girl was murdered in 1745, so the story goes. Her ghost still haunts the inn.

This print shows how the Bell Hotel in Sadler Gate looked before its dressing of timber after World War One. Originally one of Derby's major coaching inns, the Bell is haunted by several ghosts.

has nothing to substantiate it, but she has been seen on two occasions in connection with children. In the 1930s, the landlord had an asthmatic son. One afternoon he heard him coughing and choking in his bedroom. The boy's father ran upstairs and burst into the bedroom, to find a lady dressed in 18th-century costume bending his son over and patting him on the back. As the boy's father took over, the mysterious figure simply vanished before his eyes.

In the 1950s this same room was used as a nursery. One day the baby was being changed by the landlady and mother of the child. She moved away to get some nappy pins and cotton wool, and as she turned back, standing over the baby, stooping as if to pick the child up, was the same figure in the 18th-century costume, complete with mob cap. The mother rushed to pick her child up and as she did, the ghostly figure completely faded away.

Perhaps the reason that this ghost lingers here is that she died trying to protect her child, or maybe even in childbirth. Perhaps she was not a servant at all, but a dedicated nursery maid. **R.F.**

The George Inn

The shrill sound of a post horn announced the arrival of the London to Manchester coach as the tired horses picked up and flew through the streets of Derby. The large wheels clattered on the cobbles of the tiny road leading from Bold Lane to the George Inn in Iron Gate.

As the coach pulled up in the George Yard, off Sadler Gate ostlers rushed out to hold the horses, and the coachman, wrapped in large overcoats, one on top of the other, put away his whip and climbed down from the box.

Passengers going further had a little time for a meal in the coffee room. The George Yard was now as busy as a railway station at rush hour, with ostlers, coachmen and passengers going about the business of changing horses and getting the coach back on the road again within a quarter of an hour.

The George Inn was one of the most famous coaching inns in Derby and was built around 1693. By this time there was a distinction between inns and taverns, as inns were not only coaching houses, but also a place where gentlemen could stay if they did not own a townhouse in Derby. Many gentlemen certainly did stay at the George. The Duke of Devonshire frequented it on many occasions and during the 1745 Jacobite uprising, used it as his headquarters, holding

The following morning two Highland officers rode into Derby. They inquired after the mayor but he had also left the town, so they hammered on the doors of the George and demanded billets for thousands of troops.

Many other gentlemen stayed at the George during its long history. In 1763, Prince Viktor Freidrich Von Halt-Benburg stayed there for two nights. The George also played host to the Duke of York and Louis IX of Hesse, Damstadt in 1771.

Inns of the 18th and 19th century fulfilled many roles in the community, providing a place for courts, council meetings, recruiting offices, the buying and selling of animals. Doctors and dentists and vets held surgeries within the inns. In 1776, the George also took over as the post office while the one in Queen Street was being rebuilt. It also acted as a funeral parlour in 1773 when the body of Godfrey Heathcote, the Duke of Devonshire's comptroller, lay at the George *en route* for burial at Chesterfield.

the inaugural meetings which led to the formation of the regiment of soldiers called the Derby Blues.

In December 1745, the Blues held their first drill on the Holmes in Derby. They were dispatched to their billets and the duke and his officers went back to the George. At 7.30 that evening the news came that the Pretender's troops were at Ashbourne. The Duke of Devonshire held a brief council of war in the George. Would the local troops attempt to prevent the Highlanders entering Derby? After all, wasn't that why they had been formed? But no, the duke marched out of the George, took his position in front of his troops on the Market Place and gave the order: "The Derby Blues will retire". Thus they marched away towards Nottingham and left Derby to its fate.

The George, of course, has many ghosts and mysteries, none more

The George Inn, where a mysterious skull was discovered in the cellar.

bizarre than the 'George Skull'. This female human skull, with a damaged cranium, was found by workmen 4ft down in a pit beneath the cellar floor. With it were animal skulls and bones, old shoes and strips of leather. Work was stopped and the skull was taken to Nottingham for forensic testing which showed that it was very old.

Richard Felix pictured in the George cellar with the skull.

Now one's imagination can run riot. Perhaps this unfortunate female was murdered and thrown into a pit or 'midden' that would have been dug in earlier days. Animals would once have been killed on the premises to feed travellers and the unwanted parts thrown into a pit. Perhaps the woman was also thrown in there to conceal the murder.

The joint managers of the George Inn with the skull. They experienced strange happenings in the pub.

Yet no other human remains were found, other than the skull. Perhaps she was not murdered. Perhaps those workmen digging in that cellar in 1992 came across something quite different as the George stands almost on the corner of Iron Gate and Sadler Gate, the heart of Viking Derby. 'Gate' is an old Danish word for 'street'. Iron Gate was where the blacksmiths traded and Sadler Gate was where the leather workers set up business.

Perhaps a Viking leather worker's shop on the site of the George was uncovered, which would account for the shoes and the discarded leather strips. The animal bones and skulls could have come from the animals killed for the leather makers. The hides would have been stripped and tanned and the off-cuts thrown into the pit.

Maybe the damage to the side of the skull was simply done by a spade because in 1693, when the George was built, it was still customary to bury beneath the foundations of new buildings a human skull, a pair of shoes and a dead cat to ward off evil spirits and witches.

If that was the purpose for which this skull was buried, then it has not done its job very well as the George is decidedly haunted. On two occasions a long-haired man in a blue coat has been spotted walking along the landing in the middle of the night. He has been followed down the stairs into the bar where he disappeared, although there was apparently nowhere for him to go as the George was well secured. Crockery moves itself from the racks in the kitchen, but never breaks.

Since the refurbishment and extension of the cellar, bar staff have had strange experiences there: one

The skull found at the George, dramatically pictured on an executioner's block. Some folk say that the surface of the block feels slimy, as if covered in blood.

found that stainless steel buckets were being thrown at him from a table; another who went down to change the beer barrels on a Friday night had to evade the plastic taps used on the beer kegs as they were hurled at him across the cellar floor.

A disembodied human groan has been heard in the cellar and on three occasions, in the presence of customers, thick pint pots have shattered, cutting the hands of barmaids and the landlady. There has been no explanation for any of the occurrences. **R.F.**

The Greyhound

Built sometime during the 17th century, the Greyhound pub is now devoid of all its original features and there is much debate as to origin of its name. It certainly has nothing to do with the former greyhound track which was nearby at what was the old County Gaol. It was one of the few remaining public houses which served people attending the markets and horse fairs, which once took place in the area, as well as the people travelling to witness public executions at the local prisons.

Several ghosts and a haunted chair – which is believed to be cursed – exist within this popular watering hole in Friar Gate, Derby. Students from Derby University set up an investigation group in order to research alleged haunted buildings in Derby and the Greyhound, it was decided, was a likely place to start as one of the students already worked there and had heard of the pub's reputation for being haunted.

The haunted chair in the pub earned its reputation after several people noted that men, especially those with a particular Christian name, had died within a specific time after sitting in the chair.

The Greyhound in Friar Gate. The building contains a haunted chair and has been the scene of other ghostly phenomena.

According to one student the chair, which became known as the 'Chair Of Death', emitted a strange feeling which 'sensitive' individuals claimed they could feel. One lady, who claimed she was a medium, informed me that the chair is situated on the site of a gruesome murder which took place several centuries ago. Another lady informed me that the building's negative energies and 'bad vibrations' – which I was assured that all such public houses emitted – accumulated at the spot where the chair is situated; she also suggested that this is perhaps the 'heart' of the building and therefore a focal point for any such negative energies. Anyone sitting there is likely to experience ill fortune shortly afterwards.

Haunted chairs are not uncommon in supernatural lore. Indeed, the occurrence of household items being haunted

The haunted chair at the Greyhound Inn. Three men by the name of Jim sat there and soon afterwards they each died.

are on the increase. Many writers of ghost books have included whole chapters on 'Haunted Chairs', including the famous ghost hunter Alisdair Mac-Gregor in his book *Phantom Footsteps* (1959), in which he discusses several such notable cases of spirits who still hold fast to earthly belongings.

Two Derby students who decided to 'stake out' the Greyhound told of how they had remained locked in the public house one night and had encountered footsteps within the building in the early hours of the morning, when there were no other people present but themselves. Other noises including scratching and knocking sounds were heard coming from several locations within the building.

One student took a casual photograph of the inside of the building. When developed the picture revealed a misty substance in which appeared to be seated a lady with a pleasing countenance and old-style dress. This 'ghost' had, on numerous occasions, also been observed wandering the building by several members of staff and customers.

Staff also claimed that weird and curious happenings regularly occurred in many parts of the pub, including beer bottles regularly being moved, blasts of freezing cold air on relatively warm days being experienced within the building, strange figures which mysteriously appeared and as quickly vanished again. Beer pumps being switched off when they had been switched on only five minutes before, a man in a hat and a strange sweet smell in the rear area of the building have also been experienced.

Scratched into a window pane on the front of the building, is some unusual writing which is said to have been carved into the glass by criminals who were taken to the pub as their last wish before execution or long-term sentences. There is much debate as to the validity of such incidents happening but from recorded history we do know that prisoners were often released to buy food as long as they returned at a specified time.

The ghost of the man who is said to have carved the writing is believed to haunt the building. Also present within this building is a bricked-up doorway, which is believed by many to be a secret passageway which leads directly to the old Borough Gaol prison which was situated just across the road in Friar Gate, where the Howard Hotel now stands.

Regardless of the ghosts which haunt the Greyhound, the building remains a popular social focus for many people in the area, who claim that the ghosts only serve to add to the building's charm. **W.A.**

Ye Olde Spa Inne

Around 1773, a Dr Chauncey came across a mineral spring just off Abbey Street, Derby. Chauncey was an entrepreneur and seized the opportunity to rival places like Buxton and Bath. Simpson's *History of Derby* states: 'He put down a basin into the spring of it, to come out fresh: he built a cover over the spring which discharges itself by a grate and keeps the place always dry. About 20 yards below the spa he made a handsome cold bath and some rooms to it at considerable expense.'

Apparently Chauncey was only exploiting something which was already well-known. In 1611, the burgesses of Derby were already receiving rent for 'a watering place at the nether edge of Abbie Barne', so it appears that the commercial properties of the spring had been realised for at least 120 years before he decided to capitalise on them. Unfortunately Dr Chauncey died in 1736, and his spa seems to have died with him.

A double-gabled cottage was built on the site of the spa. It then became a farm and in the 19th century, a public house, which is what stands there today.

The buildings appear to be haunted, but whether by the ghost of Dr Chauncey, no one seems to know. On frequent occasions the landlord has sensed that he is not alone in the cellars, and on three occasions his name has been called by a strange voice when there is no one else there. **R.F.**

Ye Olde Spa Inne, Abbey Street. A ghostly voice has been heard in the cellar and one landlord felt he was not alone down there.

The Seven Stars

In 1693, Derby had 694 families, 76 malthouses, and 120 ale houses – nearly one pub for every 35 people. Malting was one of the main occupations within the town and the beer was so good that 'Darby ale houses' were opened in London. Malting is an occupation that dates back to before the Romans came to Britain and nearly all inns and ale houses brewed their own ale. One of the last to do this before the current trend of 'micro-breweries' attached to pubs – was the Seven Stars in King Street. The pub dates back to 1680 and is built on the site of the Augustinian monastery of St Helen's.

The Seven Stars was once run by a Mrs Henry and her son, Phil. On one

The Seven Stars public house. One landlady was locking up for the night when she saw a cloaked figure walk through a wall there.

occasion, when it was Phil's night off, Mrs Henry was locking up and as she closed the shutters she looked down a corridor and saw what she thought was a man who had taken a wrong turning. She called out: "I've locked up at the back, you'll have to come this way." She walked along the corridor to where the grey cloaked man was standing, but to her horror the figure vanished through a wall. Phil Henry arrived home to find his mother sobbing and distraught.

After she had described what she had seen, Phil decided to investigate the history of the building. It appears that centuries ago, a monk travelled to Derby and knocked on the door of the Seven Stars. The landlord, by law or custom, should have offered him sustenance but instead he refused. Legend has it that the monk collapsed in the snow and that his ghostly figure still haunts the Seven Stars where he was refused comfort centuries ago.   **R.F.**

The Noah's Ark

One particularly industrious person who used the River Derwent in the 17th century was a gentleman by the name of Noah Bullock, who built an 'ark' and moored it on the Derwent near the Morledge. He lived on it with his wife, five daughters and four sons whom he named Shem, Ham, Japhet and Benjamin. His religious devotion ended there, however, as Bullock's occupation aboard his floating home was the coining of counterfeit money.

In 1676 his crime – a capital offence in those days – was discovered and Bullock appeared before the Recorder of Derby, Sir Simon Degge, whom Noah knew well. The forger promised to end his activities, broke up his ark and sank it in the River Derwent, thus escaping the hangman. Today there is a public house in the Morledge bearing the name of Noah's Ark, a link with a notorious Derby character from the 17th century, who is said to haunt the pub.

Close to the site where Noah Bullock may have built, moored and eventually sank his ark, several river ghosts and strange lights which erratically move and twist in a strange dance have been seen. There is no explanation for these lights, apart from one medium who claims that they are the lost souls of the dead seeking a pathway to the next life.

R.F.

The Wardwick Tavern

If one wants to see a really unspoilt, original example of an 18th-century Derby gentleman's town house, than one should look no further than the Wardwick Tavern, opposite Derby Museum. The building looks practically the same today as it did when it was built for Samuel Allsop in 1712. Mercifully, it has completely escaped the shop-fronting which has scarred so many important buildings in the centre of Derby and other towns.

The building retains its carriage entrance under a huge oak beam which leads to an enchanting cobbled courtyard. At the back of the pub once stood Allsop's Brewery. Over the

The Wardwick Tavern, formerly Samuel Allsopp's house. Various ghosts are connected with this magnificent example of an 18th-century Derby gentleman's town house.

last century the pavement and road level of the Wardwick has been raised so much that a plaque on the wall of the Wardwick Tavern, recording the height of the Derby flood of April 1842, seems rather low today. The floods happened on April Fool's Day and lives were lost because the townspeople did not believe the watchman's warnings.

There are various ghosts in the old Wardwick Tavern. The landlady, Sally, has seen a strange figure standing in the extensive cellars below the building and the pub's glass-washing machine frequently switches itself off without human interference. **R.F.**

Georgian House Hotel

This building in Friar Gate is believed to have been built for a naval officer who served under Admiral Nelson. It was also the residence of a governor of the old Derbyshire County Gaol in Vernon Street and the ghostly figure of a man dressed in a blue suit has often been seen standing in the area of the hallway and also on the stairs.

R.F.

Curiouser and Curiouser

Radiants

There are many reported accounts of people having experienced the curious visitations of spirit children which mysteriously appear, often in the early hours of the morning, usually when the observer is rousing from sleep.

Several reports of these ghostly children circulate throughout Derbyshire. Their appearance, according to local legend, are said to be an omen of some forthcoming disaster or misfortune for the beholder of the vision. These spectral children are referred to by many ghost researchers as 'Radiants', or 'Invisibles', although the title Invisibles is more commonly used to refer to the invisible playmates which many children claim to have as friends. Some schools of thought dismiss these figures as pure figments of the imagination. However, it has been suggested by many researchers that most children have an inherent power to see ghosts which the onset of maturity and the development of scepticism destroys. Research into this subject has been conducted by the Religious Experience Unit at Oxford University.

Radiants, however, can appear at anytime. They are always described as golden-haired children which seem to exude a radiance or glow from their ghostly, often diaphanous bodies.

Several of these spirits have been seen in the vicinity of former workhouses and mills, especially Arkwright's Mill at Cromford. Several other mills in Derbyshire are also said to be haunted and there are numerous accounts of these ghostly children being seen. It is a fact that children were employed at these mills, frequently being mistreated, often losing limbs in the machinery, and undoubtedly many of them were probably killed or died from diseases they caught through unsanitary living conditions. Children as young as ten were often given so called 'apprenticeships'. These children were made to work up to 16 hours a day, seven days of the week, with little more to survive on than watery gruel, a few potatoes and occasionally black bread. There is documented evidence that children as young as three and four years of age were employed in such mills in the 18th century.

Many people believe Radiants to be the unsettled spirits of children who died in some unfortunate or mysterious way.

Of the many stories throughout Derbyshire, none seems more popular than the golden-haired boy seen in the foundations of the former William & Glyn's Bank, in Derby, which was rebuilt as the Royal Bank of Scotland where the Cornmarket meets the Market Place and which was previously the site of John Smith's clock shop. This ghost child was seen by a labourer who was digging through the old foundations. See *Ghost Child in the Foundations* later in this chapter.

There was also a golden-haired girl who appeared on several occasions to a lady living at Duffield. The lady was later to discover, through a neighbour and after seeing a picture of the child, that a girl had died in the house under tragic circumstances. There are also dozens of other accounts by ordinary people who claim to have seen spirit children, some on more than one occasion.

Researchers have spent a great deal of time trying to solve the mystery of why so many people have exper-

A Duffield lady was to discover, through a neighbour and after seeing this picture of a child, that the girl had died in her house under tragic circumstances.

ienced these ghostly children. Some say that they are angels who protect those to whom they appear. Others claim that they are children who died under tragic circumstances and cannot accept their deaths. Many people still believe them to be ill omens. **W.A.**

Boundary Road

At the junction of Boundary Road and Uttoxeter Road stands a graveyard which has long been reputed to be haunted. Several ghosts are said to haunt the vicinity, but perhaps the best known is a crying ghost said to be that of a young woman.

One gentleman, Adrian, an extremely down-to-earth young man on his way home from Derby city centre late one night, experienced the following incident and although it is not connected to the crying ghost of the graveyard, it may still be of interest to some readers.

"Having arrived at the Boundary Road junction, I turned the corner and, out of the corner of my eye I could see movement coming from behind the iron railings on top of the wall which surrounds the graveyard. Suddenly, and without warning, there was a distinct sound of something moving quickly about my head.

"It was all I could do to keep on walking and as soon as I felt able, I began to run as fast as I could. On arriving home I tried to rationalise what I had experienced – was it a bat or a bird and had I perhaps panicked? I knew that this was not true because

Uttoxeter Road Cemetery at the junction with Boundary Road. One young man, walking home late one night, had a scare here.

I had frequently passed the graveyard and never been bothered by it before – but the more I thought about it, the more I became convinced that I had in some way come into contact with some sort of invisible ghost." **W.A.**

The Headless Cross

Derby suffered several times from the plague, perhaps being worst affected in 1592 when 464 people perished. Local farmers refused to trade with the townspeople and it is said that grass grew in the Market Place from lack of people and business.

As the plague continued, it was feared that there would be a famine until, at last, farmers in the surrounding countryside agreed to trade with the people of the town under the condition that money for the payment of provisions was left in bowls of vinegar at the Headless Cross on Nun's Green. The farmers returned later to collect their money.

The 'Hedles Cros', or 'Broken Crosse', as it has been recorded, is thought to date from the 14th century and by the 15th it had been recorded as already having lost its top. At one time the cross was moved to the Derby Arboretum park, where it stood for many years, having a reputation even then of being haunted. Eventually the Headless Cross was moved back to the top of Friar Gate, probably quite close to where it originally stood.

Two ghosts have been seen near the

The Headless Cross in Friar Gate, where money was left to 'disinfect' in vinegar during the plague. A woman is said to haunt the area and the cross is said to emit 'an eerie feeling'.

Headless Cross, one of which is said to be that of a dog sitting. The other is alleged to be the figure of a lady in grey – although she is sometimes in white – 'coming out of the stone'. Some claim that the ghost of another lady which is often seen on the Arboretum is in some way connected with the cross, whilst others believe that the same ghost now haunts both Friar Gate and the Arboretum park.

W.A.

The Metro Cinema

Having originally served as a school and built in the latter half of the 19th century, this Gothic style building in Green Lane now functions as a cinema and college and is reputed to be haunted by two ghosts. The first is said to be that of a former janitor who committed suicide in the rear of the building. Several people have experienced feeling uncomfortable in the cellar regions of the college, whilst others have met with sudden icy blasts of air and abnormal cold spots. The second ghost is said to be that of a small boy who has been seen upstairs in the building. This ghost, however, is said to be mostly quiet and melancholy in appearance but occasionally he is heard crying and, from time to time, laughing.

W.A.

The Phantom Coach

At the back of Sadler Gate is a narrow cobbled lane – the George Yard – which leads behind the shops before emerging once again at the bottom of Sadler Gate. It is here that a ghostly carriage has been seen slowly moving down the cobbled lane.

Perhaps there is a connection with The George public house where a skull was unearthed; perhaps the coach is part of some ghostly re-enactment, the meaning of we have yet to discover. Close to this cobbled lane is a bricked and barred window which many people claim emits a strange and sinister feeling. One lady medium claimed that at one time, a gruesome murder has taken place there, but for now the window will remain a curious mystery.

W.A.

Haunted Arboretum

Opened in 1840 and bequeathed to the town by local philanthropist Joseph Strutt, Derby Arboretum was England's first public park. It was

The Arboretum bandstand. Music has been heard when no band has been present.

The Arboretum where many ghosts are said to haunt, including those of a crying child, a grey lady and the appearance of a ball of fire.

The ghost of the grey lady has been seen near this summer house at the Arboretum.

The ghost which is said to haunt the vicinity most frequently is that of yet another 'grey lady', who has frequently been seen walking away from the direction of the Royal Crown Derby china factory which backs on to the Arboretum from Osmaston Road.

One account of the grey lady comes from a man called David who, as a child, lived in the area. He told me: "As children, me and my brother used to scare each other with ghost stories. There were many occasions when we heard stories from friends and relatives about ghosts, especially about the grey lady. Several of our friends claimed to have seen her wandering the grounds of the Arboretum.

"There were many other ghost stories connected to the area but none held as much fascination and mystery as the grey lady. In fact, every other street in the area seemed to have a haunted house including one in particular, now demolished, which we used to call the 'witches' house' which stood behind the Reginald Street swimming baths.

"This house was also said to be haunted by a grey lady, only this time she was quite sinister and evil in appearance with warts and hair on her chin, unlike the lady in the park who was said to be young and beautiful.

"One night me and my brother and several friends decided to sneak out when our parents thought we were in

designed by John Claudius Loudon and its opening attracted thousands of people from all over the Midlands who travelled to Derby by steam train and horse-drawn carriages.

The Arboretum is said to to be haunted by several ghosts, one in particular 'terrifying in appearance', being 'non human' and 'not of this world'. Another ghost, heard crying, is thought to be that of a child, whilst another is a man in a hat and dark uniform believed to be a former park attendant.

A former lodge near Reginald Street was referred to by local children as the 'Ghost House' after the regular appearance of a sad young man with fair hair, looking out of a window.

The ghost of a 'grey lady' has frequently been seen walking away from the direction of the Royal Crown Derby china factory which backs on to the Arboretum from Osmaston Road.

bed, in search of the grey lady. It was a warm night and we all met at the park gates on Reginald Street at 11.45pm, as the clock on Reginald Street swimming baths indicated. I was 17 at the time and my brother was 14. Our friends were all around the same age, although my brother was the youngest.

"We had all been laughing and joking about the grey lady and ghosts in general, hidden as we were within bushes close to the gates of the park. We watched the hands of the swimming baths clock reach midnight and then we all turned our attention to the hillocks within the park where the grey lady had apparently frequently been seen.

"The lamps in the park cast an eerie glow and then, where there had previously been nothing, a misty figure in grey appeared, some 200 to 300 yards away from where we were hiding in the bushes.

At first it appeared to be formless, like a mist which moved slowly amongst the hillocks and trees. As we all watched transfixed, the figure became clearer, we could all see that the figure was indeed the grey lady.

"She appeared to be young, although her features seemed blurred, yet at the same time her face seemed to glow with a peculiar radiance. The lady moved amongst the trees and hillocks in a haphazard way, seeming to lack direction or pattern until, quite suddenly, her direction changed and she began walking directly towards us.

"At that moment we all panicked as we realised that she was approaching where we were hidden and, needless to say, we were all terrified and ran away.

"Once outside the park, we looked back to see that she was no longer there. This seemed even more terrifying. We laughed nervously and chattered for several minutes, then we ran home to our safe and warm beds. Weeks later I got a good telling off from my parents when my brother, who had been so terrified by the experience, told my mother what we had been up to."

Gerald, also once a local of the area, recounted a terrifying experience he had whilst taking a short cut through the park from Normanton Road to Reginald Street. He was confronted by what he described as a 'ball of fire'.

"It was orange in colour, about three feet in width and rolled across the hills towards me." He was so

The Arboretum is said to to be haunted by several ghosts, one in particular of 'terrifying appearance',

terrified that he began to run but it seemed that the faster he ran, the faster the ball of fire came after him until he had left the park and, looking back, could no longer see it.

Another haunted area of the park is the bandstand, still occasionally used, where ghostly music, it has been said, emanates from the inside of the building, often in the early hours of the morning, although one lady claims to have heard the phantom music on a sunny Sunday morning. The original bandstand was bombed during World War Two, together with two houses in Shaftesbury Street.

Several properties in the vicinity of the Arboretum park are said to be haunted, including a large house on Rose Hill Street where the phantom figure of an old man was seen regularly at the same window for several decades. There was also a house in Arboretum Square where an occupier, Jackie Hemingway, regul-arly witnessed a figure 'like a dress-maker's mannequin' pass through her bedroom and disappear through a wall. **W.A.**

Reginald Street

Running parallel to the Arboretum park is Reginald Street, the scene of several hauntings. The swimming baths were built in the 19th century and finally closed their doors in 1982 due to lack of use and deterioration. The building has since undergone conversion and is now a retirement home.

The slipper baths, which once stood either side of the main building but are now demolished, were said to have been haunted by the ghost of a man who had committed suicide there. Several people claim to have heard choking noises coming from the vicinity of the male slipper baths. One lady, Mrs Oddy, claimed that, one night in winter whilst walking home with her boyfriend, a man wearing a blood-stained shirt lunged towards her then vanished.

Another Reginald Street building known to be haunted was one which was used as a dental technicians and where poltergeist phenomena were experienced in the early 1970s. It was alleged that many strange things happened at the dental lab including false teeth being moved around, false teeth being placed on an assistant's shoulder, bizarre noises, odd figures and, the strangest incident of all, when a padlock and chain, placed on the central gates the night before, was found the following morning wrapped around and securely attached to a cat's neck. So concerned were the workers there that they eventually called in the local vicar from St James's Church. After the vicar had performed an exorcism on the building the poltergeist activity mysteriously stopped.

Another dental technicians, also haunted by a poltergeist, stood on Osmaston Road, near the Eagle Centre, where dental surgeons arriving for work one morning discovered an apple with dozens of teeth embedded in it.   **W.A.**

Ghost Child in the Foundations

When the previous building on the site of what is now the Royal Bank of Scotland in the Cornmarket was being demolished in the early 1970s,

When a bank was built on the site of the former clock shop (pictured right) at the junction of the Market Place and the Cornmarket, a workman saw the ghost of a child as he dug out the foundations.

the *Derby Evening Telegraph* reported that a workman was alone in what was left of the cellars when he looked up to see a little boy in rags, alone, sitting upon a ledge above him.

The workman asked the boy what he was doing there. The child replied: "I've come from the inn,"

Originally the old Tiger Inn was situated, not where it is now, at the back of Lock-Up Yard, but fronting the Cornmarket next to where the little boy was seen. This boy has also been seen on the other side of the Royal Bank of Scotland in the cellar beneath the Acropolis Café. Ladies who work there have seen a little boy sitting crying on the cellar steps and presumed that he was trapped in their cellar. Cleaners at the Royal Bank of Scotland have also seen the little boy in the basement, others have heard him crying. Lights go on and off, tills open and close, lockers with no keys lock themselves, and many people who work at the Royal Bank of Scotland have experienced the presence of this little boy.

Tunnels beneath the Lock-Up Yard. The ghost of a small boy was seen near here when a bank was being built.

Many years ago, where the Kardomah Café stood, a lady was cooking breakfast in the kitchens and looked down into Lock-Up Yard and saw a little boy in rags sitting on the pavement. She waved to him and he waved back. She went to fetch some workmates to have a look at the child in rags, but when she returned with them, he was nowhere to be seen. **R.F.**

Friar Gate Bridge

Friar Gate Bridge was built between 1876 and 1878, when the Great Northern Railway came to Derby. This particular line made a considerable impact on the Derby townscape, gouging its way through the north and west sides of the town, going through Little Chester and crossing the River Derwent. It cut through streets and destroyed buildings. Imagine the public outcry at the time – a railway line passing through Friar Gate, Derby's most elegant Georgian thoroughfare.

Arguments against it were put forward but to no avail, and in 1877 a fine cast-iron bridge was constructed over Friar Gate to link up with the GNR's Friar Gate Station, which had subterranean passages and stairs to elevated platforms.

The job of manufacturing the bridge was given to Andrew Handyside, a Scot who, in 1844, had taken over the Duke Street foundries of Messrs Weatherhead & Glover. Handyside built many bridges throughout the world but his masterpiece has to have been Friar Gate Bridge, possibly the most elaborate and ornamental railway bridge in the country, with Derby's coat-of-arms incorporated into the finely decorated panels.

One of the major casualties caused by the building of the bridge was the demolition of the White Horse Inn, a

Friar Gate Bridge, over which people say they have seen a ghostly steam train thunder.

medieval thatched building which stood directly in the path of the railway. A phantom steam train has been reported to have been seen passing over the bridge. Perhaps it is packed, as it may well have been a century ago – even 40 years ago – with excited holidaymakers on their annual trip to Skegness and Mablethorpe. **R.F.**

Glossary of Ghosts and Terminology

Animal Ghosts

Many experts on the supernatural agree that animal ghosts do exist and believe that the spirits of animals also survive the death process. There are many books which specifically deal with the issue of animal ghosts, perhaps the most recognised one being written by ghost hunter Elliott O'Donnell, who says in his book *Animal Ghosts* (1913): 'The mere fact that there are manifestations of "dead" people proves some kind of life after death for human beings; and happily the same proof is available with regard for a future life for animals; indeed there are as many animal phantoms as human – perhaps more.'

There is also a school of thought which believes that animals have what is known as a 'collective soul'. This suggests that five, or even more animals at one time, may share one soul. This may be hard to believe, but the theosophical implications of what a shared soul could possibly mean are indeed enormous.

Apparition

An apparition is said to be the ghost of someone the person seeing it knows, or a ghost which appears in human shape, looking and appearing as if it were alive but was in fact long dead.

The tradition of apparitions goes back to the earliest of times and documented accounts are numerous in the pages of history. Some apparitions are known to appear when only some disaster is about to happen, whilst there are those which are known to guard sacred places. Apparitions are not always visual, they are often heard or felt.

Banshee

The banshee, or 'bean si', as this spirit should be correctly pronounced, is undoubtedly Ireland's most famous ghost. Said to follow ancient Irish families, she is more likely to be seen by a third daughter and is more commonly said to follow a family if the first letter of their surname is 'O'.

She is said to appear prior to the death of a family member and announces the death by crying and wailing during the night hours. The sound which she emits, is said to be like that of two cats fighting only much worse. She is known to cry about the death of a relative who is thousands of miles away in another country, and is reported to appear several nights in succession until the actual death occurs. She is often described as being small, appearing either as a horrible hag dressed in rags who sometimes emits a strange smell, or as a young and beautiful woman dressed in a green dress. The eyes are always said to be red and swollen from constant crying. There is a third type, but no one knows whether she is young or old, as she has no clear features, often being described as having holes where her eyes and nose should be. All three types are described as having very long hair which streams out in the wind. If the banshee is disturbed by a mortal she will not appear again whilst that generation lives, but will return to haunt future generations.

Boggart

The name boggart is a word mainly used in the North of England and is used to describe a particularly nasty type of ghost. Boggarts are said to have a habit of crawling into people's bedrooms at night and pulling the bedclothes off, pinching, slapping, and biting, especially feet. Those unlucky enough to see one will get a shock, for they are said to be fearsome looking with sharp, bright, long and yellowing teeth.

Bogie

The bogie is a rather unpleasant spirit and especially favours haunting children hence, 'If you don't stop being naughty the bogie man will get you!' According to British folklore, bogies are black in appearance, have ugly grinning faces and are short and hairy with a foul smell about them. They were once thought to be the most powerful amongst ghosts for they had once served the Devil by doing evil deeds against mankind. They have been known to make wailing noises, in the wind, similar to the Irish banshee.

Birds

There are many instances of birds returning as ghosts. Birds were at one time believed to be messengers of the dead and when a bird often tapped on a window it was looked upon as meaning that a ghost was looking for another spirit to join it. Certain birds, sparrows, larks and storks, were said to carry the souls of people from the Guff (Hall Of Souls) in Heaven, to earth. Other birds, more specifically crows, were believed to carry the spirits of humans onto the next plain of existence.

Cats

Said to be the most common form of animal haunting next to dogs. The ghost cat is believed to have its spooky origin in ancient Egypt where cats were often worshipped especially at Bubastis, where many thousands of mummified cats have been excavated.

Historically the Devil was believed to be able take the form of a cat. Elliot O'Donnell in his *Occult Review* (1962), reports: 'There are, at the present moment, many houses in England haunted by phantoms in the form of black cats, of so sinister and hostile an appearance, that one can only assume that unless they are the actual spirits of cats, earthbound by cruel and vicious propensities, they must be vice elementals, *i.e.* spirits that have never inhabited any material body, and which have either been generated by vicious thoughts, or else have been attracted elsewhere to a spot by some crime or vicious act once perpetrated there.'

Clairaudiant

The ability to hear disembodied voices of the dead, or other entities, who normally tell of events yet to happen. Many mediums claim the ability to hear dead relatives and pass on information from a place they call the 'Spirit World'.

Clairsentient

An ability to be able to feel things in a divinitory sense. To know things which have been, are, and are yet to be. Those who claim to have this ability state that it is basic human instinct finely attuned and polished.

Clairvoyant

The ability claimed by some to be able to see visions of events yet to happen, happening, or that have happened. This word in its simplest form basically means 'to see with sight beyond the normal human range of sight'.

Crossroad Ghosts

Crossroads have long been associated with hauntings, and although it is not clear as to exactly why, some interesting theories are still to be found. Ghost hunter Elliot O'Donnell in his book *Haunted Britain* (1948) suggests the following: Some think it is because in olden times, murderers, sorcerers and suicides were buried at crossroads, with a stake thrust through them in a foolishly vain attempt to keep their spirits from wandering; others think it is because witches and wizards were believed to hold orgies and practise the Black Art at crossroads; while others, again, think crossroads, like lonely pools, old quarries and some woods, have a peculiar attraction for a certain species of spirits.'

Other researchers maintain that crossroads are more likely to be haunted because of the amount of suicides which were buried there. The superstition of interring the dead at such places lies in the Christian belief of the cross being a form of protection from demons, vampires and such supernatural night creatures. This, however, is thrown into doubt when we consider that excavated human remains near crossroads and predating Christianity have been unearthed all over the world.

Deathwatch
This strange turn of phrase is connected to a species of beetle known as the deathwatch beetle which taps on wood. It was believed by many that the beetle could sense the presence of death and tapped in acknowledgement of spirits arriving to take the soul to its next destination.

Dogs
Ghost dogs are reported all over the British Isles and are said to vary in size. They can be small with extremely large eyes, be white, black, vicious or of a gentle disposition. In Lancashire they have a ghost dog known as a Striker, in Wales there is the Gwyllgi, whilst here in Derbyshire we have the Rach Hounds and Gabriel's Ghost Hounds which are often heard in or near Chesterfield.

Doppelganger
The word is derived from German and is an expression for a ghost which is actually the double of a living person. Those who experience seeing their double are said to be heading towards misfortune in the near future. Some writers maintain that the doppelganger can also be an indication of good fortune, although recorded incidents of them being good omens are rare. They are alleged to be in every way like the person that they are haunting, being as their twin. Other people associated with the haunted individual are also reported as having seen the doppelganger at a place where the living counterpart was nowhere near.

Drude
The drude is an ancient English expression for a nightmare ghost which a mature witch or wizard, well versed in the art of magic, who is said to be able to inflict a ghost into the dreams and nightmare's of their chosen victim.

Duppy
The duppy is a well-known West Indian ghost which can be summoned from its grave to do the bidding of a witch by certain ceremonial magic which involves mixing blood and rum, together with several other substances. This is then thrown on to the grave of one known to have been an evil person when alive, as the duppy is believed by many to be the personification of evil in a human. The duppy is said to be only able to walk the earth between the hours of dusk to cock-crow.

Ectoplasm
This strange substance is said to be extruded from the sweat glands, mouth,

nostrils and genitals of certain mediums whilst in a trance-like state.

The word Ectoplasm, or Teleplasm, as it is now frequently referred to as being, is derived from the Greek word *ektos* and *plasma*, meaning exteriorised substance. Some researcher's claim that the substance is not unlike pale white tissue paper, cheesecloth, fine silk strands which all gather together to make a human shape. Other schools of thought insist that the substance is like human and animal tissue and several investigators claimed to have examined the substance stating that its biological chemistry is, at present, unknown to man.

Elementals

These strange ghosts are said to be spirits which have never existed in human form, unlike normal ghosts and spirits which have at one time, been and lived as a human. Occultists declare them as being ancient spirits, which predate man, which fall into four categories consisting of Earth, Air, Fire and Water. Elemental spirits are often associated with haunted stretches of woodland and rivers, mountains and valleys.

Elves

These spirits of nature are believed to be spiteful creatures and were said to be lost souls trapped between the two worlds, not evil enough to go to Hell, but not quite good enough to be accepted into Heaven.

Exorcism

An exorcism is an act of religious ceremony which expels a spirit which may have taken up residence in a house or human being. The ceremony normally consists of a priest or clergyman, who is often specially trained, and who will say prayers and repeat loud exhortations, often burning candles and sprinkling holy water whilst incense is burnt. This ritual is a modern version of the old Christian rite of excommunication, which was known as the rite of 'Bell, Book and Candle', where sinners were eliminated from further entering the faith by a priest who would ring a small bell and slam the *Holy Bible* shut, often after reading the Malediction, and extinguish the burning candles.

Modern mediums also claim to be able to perform such an act, normally without the trappings, by psychically contacting the spirit which may be causing the trouble and convincing it to move on to the next spiritual plane of existence. Many mediums believe that ghosts are spirits who have not come to terms with their passing, which may often have been untimely and tragic, or that in some way they are being held back from progression on a spiritual level by someone or, more often than not, something in this world.

Extras

This widely used term is now regularly used to describe faces, or whole images of people, who mysteriously appear on photographs. There are many instances of pictures being developed to reveal a long-dead relative, or occasionally someone who may be alive but thousands of miles away. Often the pictures show white wispy cloud-like substances out of which a face is normally starting to appear. In the early days of spirit photography (a claim to be able to photograph the dead), many alleged spirit faces were deliberately introduced into the photographs. Many acclaimed mediums of earlier days produced such photographs, which unfortunately have nearly all been proved to be fraudulent.

There are, however, a small number of photographs which defy explanation, many showing people or faces of the dead, and these pictures are believed to be genuine. One such picture was taken of a lady in blue at St Werburgh's Church,

Spondon, by a Miss Gwen Nicholls, who was casually taking photographs of the interior of the church in the mid-1970s. The strange phenomena of extras are discussed at length in Harry Price's fascinating book, *Search For The Truth: My Life Of Psychical Research* (1942).

Fairies

Fairies are said to be small, often tiny, invisible creatures. They can be of great help to those they favour or of great hindrance to those who upset them. The colour green is sacred to them and their place of abode is in the hills, valleys, amongst the trees, where there are ancient burial mounds and mysterious stone circles.

Fire Ball

Frequently reported and most commonly said to be seen in Scotland.

The fire ball is said to be a medium to large sphere which moves in a smooth and often slow way, more frequently reported near large stretches of water, although this is not always the case as in the fire ball which has been seen on the Arboretum and also those at Derby River Gardens. They are believed to be the souls of the departed returning to earth to guide the souls of the recently departed to the next world.

Galley Beggar

This is believed to be an old English ghost which is often reported in the North of England and is mentioned as far back as 1584, in Reginald Scot's work, *The Discovery of Witchcraft*. The ghost is said to be like a skeleton or is often described as barely having any flesh upon it. The name is derived from the word 'galley', meaning to frighten or terrify. This ghost may be often encountered on country roads frequently with the head tucked beneath its arm whilst emitting a terrifying scream.

Ghoul

The ghoul was at one time the common word for a ghost in Arabia. These days, however, the word is commonly used throughout the world to define a particularly nasty or often vicious looking ghost. In the Eastern world the ghoul was believed to be a spirit which looks almost human, having a terrifying face. The ghoul was believed to gain sustenance from eating human flesh, especially the flesh of corpses, hence the word ghoul is often used to describe ghosts which specifically haunt graveyards.

Graveyard Ghost

According to folklore, the first person to be buried in a churchyard was believed to return as a ghost to guard the site against the Devil. This ghost was believed to have special abilities. Because the task was so great, a black cat or dog was often buried before any human, so as it would become the guardian of the dead and remain so until the Crack of Doom.

Gremlin

Gremlins have only appeared in recent times and although the word is now widely used, it actually originated from World War Two when pilots flying dangerous missions reported seeing strange goblin-like creatures in the aircraft with them. Alasdair Alpin MacGregor in his book, *The Ghost Book* (1955), wrote: 'Members of the Royal Air Force, who participated in the Battle of Britain, have told me of them; and, although the *Oxford English Dictionary* fails to include the word, a professor at Oxford tells his friend, the eminent A.L.Rowse, that the gremlins "have been at me all my life". Gremlins certainly are here to stay as Steven Spielberg immortalised them in his highly-acclaimed films of these supernatural creatures, and now it seems not a piece of machinery can naturally go wrong without someone saying, 'there's a gremlin in the works'.

Grey Ladies

Said to originate from Tudor times when the Dissolution of the Monasteries resulted in the death of many monks and nuns who would have then been habited in grey. Many investigators of hauntings and ghosts claim that the theory of grey lady ghosts is similar to that of the white ladies.

Other investigators claim that the colour which a ghost appears is relevant to surrounding substances, wood, plaster, stone, shrubbery etc., which may be contributing to the ghosts appearance.

Hallowe'en

Originating long before the advent of Christianity, the 'Feast Of The Dead', perhaps being a better name for the night, was a time of great celebrations for our ancient pagan ancestors, who would light great bonfires across the country to summon the dead and placate them by offering burnt sacrifices, and warmth from the fires to help the ancient dead through the cold winter months.

The Christian Church moved the bonfire tradition to 5 November – to mark Guy Fawkes's fate – in hope of masking the true meaning of the night. To this day modern witches still celebrate the night on 31 October by holding feasts and performing magic rituals. According to legend, on the stroke of midnight the gates of Hell were opened by Satan himself and all the spirits of evil were set free on earth to wreak havoc. By cock-crow all evil spirits must return to Hell whose gates were shut tight at the first sight of dawn, any spirits left outside would thus be disintegrated forever.

Haunted Chairs

There are many reported instances throughout England of owners who had a particular fondness for – or who may have died in – an armchair, coming back as a ghost and being seen in that particular chair. In Derby there is a haunted chair at the Greyhound public house in Friar Gate. It is said that if you are male, have a certain name and are a certain age, then you should not sit there. Apparently, four men unfortunate enough to share these characteristics did – and shortly afterwards each one died.

Haunting

This word is used to describe a ghost which is seen on more than one occasion within the same building or at the same place. Therefore, when a ghost, or ghosts, are seen at the same place on successive occasions, we refer to the place as being haunted. People can also be haunted as can any item which may have belonged to someone deceased.

Headless Ghosts

These ghosts are believed to be the spirits of people who had died by being beheaded, although there is a wealth evidence to suggest that these types of apparitions may be connected to a far more ancient practice of beheading corpses, especially when they were in any way believed to be connected to witchcraft or sorcery.

Graves found at Little Chester revealed several such burials with decapitated heads being placed between the knees, perhaps in the feeble hope that the dead would not come back to haunt the living.

Iron

Believed by many to be a sure antidote against all kinds of bad magic and evil spirits who, it is claimed, hated the very sight of the substance.

Headless Horsemen

The headless horsemen of ghost tradition

is said to be a result of a rider who may have been ambushed and decapitated whilst riding swiftly through a wooded glade, as it is in such places that one might encounter such a spectral creature. Other theories state that the headless riders are ancient chieftains who lost their heads in battle and still wander the face of the earth seeking to find their dismembered heads. One other theory concerning headless horsemen and coach drivers is that they may of lost their heads whilst passing through coaching archways.

Lemures

Lemures is the name given to evil ghosts by the Romans, who believed that spirits of the dead often returned to haunt relatives and friends. Said to be especially active during certain months of the year, certain ceremonies to placate these spirits were often held in ancient Rome. Several elaborate funeral ceremonies could be presented to the gods to ensure that the return of the dead persons spirit would not happen.

Materialisation

The ability claimed by certain mediums to be able to bring into visible sight a spirit or ghost. One of the first recorded incidents of materialisation occurred in America in 1860, by the Fox Sisters, founders of modern day spiritualism.

Mermaid Pools

Also known as pools of doom, death pools, or black water, these often secluded ponds and lakes, are said to be haunted by a certain type of mischievous ghost. Many people claim that these places emit an uncomfortable feeling of sadness and melancholy. Most of these pools have, at some time or another, been reputed to have had individuals drown there.

Ouija Board

Consisting of 38 pieces of card, normally arranged around a table, each card has a different letter of the alphabet written upon it, whilst upon nine others are written the numbers zero to nine and upon two other cards the words 'yes' and 'no'. The Ouija, or Wee Gee board, as it is now so often called, is alleged to be a mediator between the world of the living and that of the dead. When all the necessary arrangements are made, and the required amount of people are present, a glass beaker or wine glass is placed on the table and the consultation with the board can begin.

Perfumed Ghosts

Some investigators in the paranormal maintain that a ghost can manifest itself in the form of a scent. Many people have experienced smelling a perfume which may have been a favourite scent of a deceased relative, such as an aunt or grandmother. Other smells are said to be horrible such as fish, faeces, burning etc. The most famous local case is one which happened in Derbyshire and was recounted in a letter sent by a Dr James Clegg in 1745, to a colleague, the Revd Dr Ebenezer Latham: 'I know you are pleased with anything curious or uncommon in Nature, and if what follows shall appear such I can assure you from eye witnesses of the truth of every particular. In a church at about three miles distance from us, the indecent custom still prevails of burying the dead in a place set apart for the devotions of the living; yet the parish not being very populous, one would scarce imagine the inhabitants of the grave could be strai'tned for want of room; yet it should seem so, for on the last of August, several hundreds of bodies rose out of the grave in the open day in that church, to the great astonishment and fear of several spectators.

'They deserted the coffin, and arising out of the grave, immediately ascended directly towards heaven, singing in concert all along as they mounted thro' the air; they had no winding sheets about them, yet did not appear quite naked, their vesture seem'd streaked with gold, interlaced with sable, skirted with white, yet thought to be exceeding light by the agility of their-motions, and the swiftness of their ascent.

They left a most fragrant and delicious odour behind them, but were quickly out of sight, and what is become of them or in what distant regions of this vast system they have since fixed their residence, no mortal can tell.

'The church is in Hayfield, three miles from Chappell Frith. 1745.'

Phantom Coaches

Also known as death's messenger, the phantom coach is believed by many to be seen prior to a death in the family of the person seeing it. The coaches are said to always be black and can be either a genuine coach or a hearse, the horses are always said to be headless, and the driver, when his features are clear, is more often than not said to be skeletal, or hideously ugly, with a fixed grin. The coach as it passes, which is sometimes at great speed, is said to be always silent and if anyone happens to accidentally get in the way of the coach and horses they will be carried away to their doom.

Poltergeist

The word poltergeist is derived from the German verb *polter*, meaning to create noise by banging, knocking or throwing things about, and the noun *Geist*, meaning ghost. Harry Price, one of the greatest authorities on ghosts, describes beautifully the antics, and make up, of this complex and nearly always unwanted spirit in *Poltergeist Over England* (1945): 'A Poltergeist is an alleged ghost, elemental, entity, agency, secondary personality, "intelligence", "power", "spirit", "imp", or 'familiar' with certain unpleasant characteristics. Whereas the ordinary ghost of our story-books is a quiet, inoffensive, timid, noiseless, and rather benevolent spirit, with usually friendly feelings towards the incarnate occupants of any place where it has its abode, the Poltergeist is just the reverse. According to the many reports of its activities, in all lands and in all ages, the Poltergeist is mischievous, destructive, noisy, cruel, erratic, thievish, demonstrative, purposeless, cunning, unhelpful, malicious, audacious, teasing, ill disposed, spiteful, ruthless, resourceful, and vampiric. A ghost haunts, a Poltergeist infests. A ghost likes solitude, a Poltergeist prefers company. A ghost seeks the half-light; a Poltergeist will "perform" in sunlight.'

Psychic

Pertaining to the soul and mind, being a mystic, clairvoyant, telepathic etc., or having a combination of supernatural abilities which allows the individual to perceive time differently. The ability to see or sense the future, present and past. Not to be confused with the word 'spiritual' which is so often used these days to describe mediums who do not need to be psychic to be spiritual but do need to be spiritual in order to be psychic.

Psychomancy

The ancient art of reading future events by the appearance of ghosts, and spirits, and what their manifestations to the living might mean.

Salt

Believed, in ancient customs of the dead and sacred myth to be a universal antidote against all manner of witchcraft and evil spirits. Anyone carrying salt in their pockets are said to be protected, even the Devil himself would not approach anyone carrying the substance. Salt is also said to subdue wicked spirits haunting a dwelling if it is placed in each and every corner of the rooms within the building.

Seance

A seance normally involves a medium who claims to be able to contact deceased relatives, or occasionally spirit guides, and even strangers, by means of material-isation of a spirit or disembodied voices. Knocking and rapping sounds may also be apparent during a seance.

The word 'seances' is French in origin meaning 'a sitting' and there is no absolute limit as to how many people can be present, although it is generally accepted that the even numbers seem to have better results.

Spectre

Once used as another word to describe a ghost but now the word is most commonly used to describe a ghost which has been found to be faked or is explained away by natural occurrences.

Talisman

An object, charm, mascot, amulet, which can be worn, kept close to oneself, or more often than not placed near, or buried close to the home. These objects are said to have the ability to ward of evil and keep ghosts at bay.

Telepathic

The ability to read minds and know the thoughts of other people, either near, or as is often reported, at a great distance.

Trance

The ability to lower the state of consciousness, between sleeping and wakefulness, where the medium claims to be able to use their bodies as a channel for waiting spirits to use and pass information through to living relatives and friends.

Vengeful Spirits

There are many instances of ghosts returning from the dead to avenge themselves of terrible wrongs which have been done to them.

The most famous local avenging spirits are those of Allen and Clara, who were brutally murdered, by five miners at the Winnats Pass (windy gates) near Castleton, Derbyshire. Whilst in the process of eloping to get married, Allen and Clara were set upon by the miners, murdered and thrown into a mine shaft. Shortly after their deaths, strange things began to happen in the vicinity. Four of the men responsible for the murder of the two young lovers died in mysterious circumstances within a year. The fifth man eventually made a death-bed confession. Perhaps his was the worst death of the five as he was tormented by what might lie in wait for him on the other side.

Wakes

This ancient custom, almost unique to Ireland, of sitting and watching over the dead whilst vast amounts of alcohol are consumed, is a tradition in which it is believed that by consuming the alcohol it will help the spirit of the deceased on its journey to the spirit world. The use of alcohol is partly in the belief that it will help cleanse the sins of the deceased. The reasoning behind a wake lies in the ancient belief that an evil spirit may try to sneak into the body before the soul has had a chance to try its luck at Heaven's gates. Noise is created at a wake by music, singing and laughing, in the Celtic belief that such loud noises will keep evil spirits away.

Warlock

Used by many writers to describe a male

witch. Many male witches, however, would find this title insulting as the word has been used in times past to describe a traitor.

White Ladies

White ladies are seen all over the British Isles, and the Peak District has its fair share of them. They traditionally haunt castles, mansions, halls and, unusually, bridges or stretches of water. The reason for white ladies being seen near water, according to one writer from France, is that in ancient times pagans were said to sacrifice young ladies to river gods, thus supposedly allowing them safe passage across.

Wizard

A person with amazing abilities, one normally well versed in the art of magic. Most male witches prefer this title.

Wraiths

According to old traditions, a wraith is a ghost of a person on the verge of death and often appears as an exact likeness of their human counterpart. They are regarded as a death omen and should a person see a wraith of themselves, then their days are numbered.

The most famous instance of an individual seeing a wraith was the poet Percy Shelley, (1792 -1822), who saw his own wraith as he stepped on to a small boat which was to take him across the Bay of Spezia in Italy. Shelley had arranged to meet with his friend, Leigh Hunt, and was eager to see him again. Needless to say, the boat foundered in the storm, Shelley was drowned and the omen of the wraith was fulfilled.

Will-o'-the-Wisp

Also known as jack-o-lantern, ignis fatuus, corpse candle, foolish fire, etc. There are many reports of this phenomenon in Derbyshire, Stanton Moor, the Weaver Hills, Monsal Dale, and anywhere near marshland. Traditionally these spirits were believed to guard lost treasures, buried priests, kings and places of pagan religious worship. Those foolish enough to follow these strange dancing lights were inevitably led to their deaths in marshland bogs. Legend has it that the lights were souls of dead murderers and evil people, cursed to wander the face of the earth forever, seeking to find rest and yet damned never to find peace until the end of the world.

Witch

A person, especially a woman who practises witchcraft. There are many different types of witches. Most worship nature and call upon gods and goddesses of fertility to help them in their magical undertakings. One interesting unwritten law concerning witches, is that they are forbidden from telling anyone what they are, or how they practise their art, believing that silence is power and power brings knowledge. Most modern witches would not use their abilities to harm anyone, instead choosing to help and promote human, animal and spiritual awareness of a greater wisdom of life than what is obviously apparent. A witch uses 'bad magic' on only rare occasions, as another unwritten law states that evil can only be justified if used for the greater good of the whole, making it difficult for the witch to decide how they will act when there may be a need to use bad magic.

W.A.

Bibliography

Haunted Britain Anthony D.Hippisley-Coxe (Hutchinson & Co Ltd. 1973).

Haunted Churches of England Graham J.McEwan (1989).

Haunted Derbyshire Daniel Clarence (Dalesman, 1975).

Ghosts of Derbyshire Daniel Clarence (Dalesman, 1973).

Derbyshire Traditions Daniel Clarence, (Dalesman, 1975).

Phantom Ladies Andrew Green (1977).

The Story of Eyam Plague Daniel Clarence (Bakewell & Wye Valley Press, 1983).

Celt, Druid and Culdee Isabel Hill Elder (Covenant Publishing Co Ltd. 1962).

Stone Circles of the Peak John Barnatt (Turnstone Books, 1978).

Exploring the Ancient Tracks and Mysteries of Mercia Shirley Toulson (1980).

Celtic Derbyshire Peter J.Naylor (Hall, Derby, 1983).

Roman Derby Maurice Brassington (Breedon Books, 1991).

Hanged for a Sheep E.G.Power (Scarthin Books, 1981).

Manors and Families of Derbyshire, Vols One & Two Peter J.Naylor (Hall, Derby, 1984).

The Secret Country Janet and Colin Bord (Book Club Associates, 1976).

The Ghost Hunters Guide Peter Underwood (Blandford Press, 1986).

Bygone Derbyshire Edited by W.Andrews (1892).

May the Lord Have Mercy on Your Soul Phillip Taylor (Hall, Derby, 1989).

A Dictionary Of Ghosts Peter Haining (Hale, 1982).

Lord Halifax's Ghost Book (London, 1936).

The Ghost Book Alisdair Alpin MacGregor (London, 1955).

Gazetteer Of Scottish & Irish Ghosts Peter Underwood (Souvenir Press, 1985).

Derby Evening Telegraph Various articles written by Anton Rippon, 1978-82.